Among Teachers

PETER L. FENNINGER

Order this book online at www.trafford.com
or email orders@trafford.com

Most Trafford titles are also available at major online book retailers.

Printed in the United States of America.

ISBN: 978-1-4669-3335-4 (sc)
ISBN: 978-1-4669-3337-8 (hc)
ISBN: 978-1-4669-3336-1 (e)

Library of Congress Control Number: 2012909804

Trafford rev. 05/24/2012

 www.trafford.com

North America & international
toll-free: 1 888 232 4444 (USA & Canada)
phone: 250 383 6864 ♦ fax: 812 355 4082

Thanks to Jane Testerman, Stu and Jenny Wallace,
Don Murray, Jen Carpenter, and especially my wife Gwen for the
support you have given in this project.
Thanks also go to many others who have urged and encouraged.

Contents

PART III. ADDENDUM

Among Teachers: An Introduction

Teaching is the second-oldest profession in mankind. Everybody has been taught; ergo, everyone is an authority on what constitutes good teaching. Also, life's a journey through stories. We first hear them when we are very little, and then we learn to tell them. Great stories affect mankind tremendously. The good ones spring from truths and are shaped over time. The best lead mankind toward hope and salvation. Great storytellers gain respect and adoration within their worlds, and their tales gain acceptance over many generations. The great religions are full of stories leading us to spirituality. Folk tales teach basic lore while providing entertainment. Dramas, anything from children's plays in church to Broadway and Hollywood presentations, broaden our horizons as they entertain. The news media provides stories of all sorts. In fact, we sometimes become overwhelmed by all the tales we hear and are forced to evaluate.

Teachers by profession are storytellers, and over time good teachers become great storytellers. They provide tales to present course material, to give examples of good behavior, and to provide a means of team building. Even the sternest teacher has good stories at his fingertips to make points. We learn through those stories, and we remember them. Our lives become better because of them.

I have spent my lifetime among teachers. Like the majority of kids in this country, I went to school through twelfth grade. Then

I went on to college and graduate school. All along the way, I met teachers of varying abilities, interests, and energy levels. But then, I decided to become a teacher myself. I have taught students at every level from third grade through community college. In the process I have had countless colleagues. Some were role models, and some became lifelong friends. Many amazed me in that they taught in ways I had never thought of and got really strong results. Some I never got to know very well; some I grew to despise. In any case, I realize that any evaluation of a teacher is subjective, and others may well see specific instructors very differently from the way I have. So be it.

I have lived for nearly seventy years and have taught for about forty of those. Even during those times when I was occupied outside the realm of formal education, I was teaching peers or employees how to complete tasks better. Each group has presented a different challenge and has caused me to experiment and grow. Furthermore, the world has changed dramatically in that time. So have teaching methods and strategies. What follows is my view of teaching and some of the stories I've encountered in that world. I am deliberately omitting names of schools and changing names of ineffective teachers because I have no wish to harm any institution or individual. I do wish to comment on the progress of teaching in a world buffeted by change.

This story is told chronologically, and pretty typically, I begin chapters with a brief review of what transpired during a decade. I've recalled from my memory rather than to document from historical documents because I have wanted this narrative to be personal rather than factually correct. Stories involve people in ways meaningful to individuals while historical tomes present events about leaders and great masses of people. Yes, education in this country is a mass thing, but it is the individual who must be affected daily in the classroom if we are to move forward as a people. That process, then, ultimately lies in the relationship between each teacher and each student. Unfortunately, that pattern is too often adversely affected by movements and issues impacting large numbers of people. No instructional situation lives in a vacuum; hence, we cannot ignore the large issues, but each teacher has to temper each student relationship with his interpretation of that issue.

So sit back and enjoy my story and meet some of those teachers I have encountered.

Part I

The Journey

The 1940s: The Beginning

The first place I remember living in is an old farmhouse outside Springtown, Pennsylvania. As is the case of most, my first teachers were my parents. Both were bright, creative, educated people who were fascinated by all around them, and they read everything in sight. The only room in our house without books was the dining room, and frequently my father would leave the table to find a passage he wanted to read to us. My mother, who might well have had a photographic memory, would recite stuff she had read years earlier. As children, we knew all the area bookstores and libraries intimately. Both our parents wrote exceedingly well, although with very different styles; thus, words and word usage were very important concepts in our growing up. My mother, particularly, insisted upon proper pronunciation and growth of word exploration. We read plays aloud, played word games of all sorts, and read and read and read. Sometimes Mom would be in trouble with her friends because she let us read comic books. Her response was, "I don't care what they read as long as they read."

In her quest for us to learn, Mom took us to New York City whenever she could. Frequently on days when there was no school, we ate breakfast, climbed in the car, and drove to New York. The Metropolitan Museum of Natural History was our usual goal. We'd marvel at the dinosaurs and the Hope Diamond and scads of other relics. Off to the Automat we'd go for lunch. Putting change in a slot, we'd be amazed when a piece of pie or a cup of soup would be turned loose for us. Then back to the planetarium we'd go to be star struck by the show. Immediately afterward, we'd find the car and be home for dinner. Occasionally, we went to matinees on or just off Broadway. If Dad went, we'd have lunch at a place far nicer than the Automat and then see a show. I still can see Prince Hal for Shakespeare's *Henry IV, Part I* and the Pirate King from Gilbert and Sullivan's *The Pirates of Penzance*.

Mom's sense of fun took us to Philadelphia as well. Mostly we visited Shibe Park, later Connie Mack Stadium, to see the Phillies play. Robin Roberts and Richie Ashburn became lifelong heroes, and baseball still is a main love of my life. The professional playing field was a magic carpet to us, and there was no joy greater to a young boy than watching demigods play. Baseball eventually grabbed my mother, and she became a Mets fan. We were joined at the hip by suffering through losing seasons by rooting for hapless squads, but we suffered with joy.

My parents were keenly aware and in full appreciation of the physical world around them. They created beautiful gardens, became serious students of birds and animals, and appreciated what the changing seasons brought. We walked in the woods year-round and watched as our endless string of dogs either cooled themselves or broke ice in the creek behind the house. We watched the deer move across the countryside in their quasi-nomadic pattern. We joyfully ate the fruits and vegetables of the seasons. As a result, we felt in tune with our surroundings and still appreciated the natural world.

My father was a very successful executive at Bethlehem Steel Corporation. He began his career at the Bethlehem Steel shipyard in Quincy, Massachusetts, and was brought to the home office in 1943. His innate ability and wordsmanship were both keys to his career growth, but so was his dedication to his duties. He was one of the hardest-working people I have ever encountered. Most of his peers lived in Bethlehem, and they lived a life patterned on what was expected of them. My parents had a freedom to be themselves and live a broader existence. When they bought a ratty, empty farmhouse outside of Springtown, they declared an independence from total devotion to corporate expectations. Yet they were very careful to play the corporate game to their advantage, and they were welcome in Bethlehem society. Because of their interests in everything around them, my parents' circle of friends was eclectic. People from all strata wandered through the house, bringing interesting ideas and conversations about everything. As we children were welcome participants in discussions, I learned how to talk with people from all walks of life. That skill has been very helpful in my varied career.

We learned important values as well. Lying was the worst sin of all. Stealing was a close second. Failure to respect other people and use good manners was a close third. Living up to obligations was expected. My mother referred to her discipline practices as the "clobber, clonk" method: she could clobber or clonk us whenever and wherever she felt the need. Retribution for sin was quick and sure. Dad was quieter when he disciplined, but we all knew that when his jaw began to tighten, it was time to clear out. He had big, strong hands. Neither parent was unfair or unduly physical in meting out punishment: each was teaching a lesson he or she thought necessary.

As a result, their beliefs in what was right and wrong live on with us today.

Both parents were active in the community. Dad was a charter member of the local Lions Club and a member of the school board. He was instrumental in starting a local chorus group, which sang Handel's *Messiah* many years about Christmas time. Mom was the first Brownie Scout troop leader and an active member of the flower club. Both worked diligently in local fund-raising activities, and both strived to be good neighbors. They worked hard to be active in the community and be accepted by it. They simply wanted to be good neighbors in a community they liked very much

Springtown, Pennsylvania, in the 1940s and '50s was a great place to grow up. The war was over, and enthusiasm abounded. Most of the men farmed or worked another trade, and they also held full-time jobs at Bethlehem Steel, the second-largest steel company in the world at that time, or Riegel Paper Corporation. Everybody working in the plants worked swing shifts, changing shifts weekly. Thus, some people were asleep at any given point in the day, but not at the same time week after week. The women stayed home and ran the houses and the family lives. Most everybody spoke English, but there were old-timers who spoke Pennsylvania Dutch, a variation of German. Dutch, as it was called, was commonly heard around town, and most kids could understand it.

Town values were pretty clear. People were honest. They were kind. They worked hard. They helped one another. They behaved themselves. They wanted their children to grow up to be good, hardworking people. They went to church. They supported the town and its institutions. Finally, they had fun.

Life was pretty simple. Television was just entering homes, and radio still provided the major link with the outside world. People no longer gathered around the giant radio as they had in the '30s, but kids still met for *The Lone Ranger, Sergeant King of the Yukon*, and other sources of amusement. But on the whole, kids grouped to play outdoors, and our lives were pretty active physically. We played incessant pickup baseball games, sledded down the hills, ice skated on Gutshall's pond, swam in the creek, and generally played hard. We went to Boy Scouts, Girl Scouts, and 4-H. We also did chores and had responsibilities to take care of. Generally, we roamed freely within our confines and looked to our own or peer creativity to keep us amused. Adult activities centered on church things and organizations of common interest like the Silver Creek Athletic Association, the Grange, the Minsi Trail Flower Club, the Lions Club, and others. The town's annual calendar focused on big events thrown by these various organizations.

Seeing Springtown was like wandering around in Thornton Wilder's *Our Town*, except for the dominance of the Steel, as Bethlehem Steel Corporation was called, and Riegel Paper Corporation. Kids knew one another from the beginning of school until the days they died. They dated one another and married to raise the next generation. Then the '60s hit, and everything changed.

As in every town, there were dominant characters. Some led by profession. Dr. Worrell cared for most of us. Harold Grim pumped gas. Reverend Bieber prayed over our souls. The Gutshalls and Sam

Stever sold and repaired cars. Mrs. Stever and Mrs. Balliet tried to teach us. Stoney Stoneback ran the post office and the general store. Maynard Barron painted our houses after the Herseys built them.

Of course there were pretty girls and beautiful women, and I expect that they saw cute boys and handsome men. In any case, biology rolled on, and the generations continued. They still do. Family reunions were always lively. People enjoyed their clans and the opportunities of good summer picnics where there was too much food and little drink.

Springtown sits in upper Buck County, Pennsylvania, between Riegelsville and Hellertown. Not far away are Quakertown, Bethlehem, Allentown, and Easton, mighty metropolises in comparison. About ninety miles east lies New York City, and fifty miles south is Philadelphia. Maybe the big cities dominated little towns the same way they do now, but I doubt it. Mass media had not yet given us instant access to all information, and WalMart and its culture were still far, far away.

When I started school, five contiguous local townships had their own school systems. About 1950, they agreed to consolidate to streamline costs and to build a badly needed new high school. There was cooperation between two of these townships in the education of children. As a result, most Springtown kids went to Durham School for first grade. Some went to Springtown School for second grade, but the rest of us stayed there until fourth grade, when we attended Springtown School, a little two-room schoolhouse with no indoor toilets. It was cold in Springtown in the winter, and we learned a lot about bladder control.

Durham School was a modern facility, and the teaching was pretty standard for the times. I do remember that Ms. Martin, our first-grade teacher, retired after a year with us. She wore a blue schoolmarm dress and black tied shoes virtually every day. The only other thing I remember about her is that one day she panicked. A boy in our class had had rheumatic fever, and his heart was weak. A small boy, he was not allowed to play outside with us during recesses. One pretty spring day, he escaped the confines of the classroom and joined us for a game of tag or whatever, and Ms. Martin almost had a stroke. I'm sure she feared that he would die right there on the spot. We were all summoned back to the room and lectured about the need to protect our classmate. Then Ms. Martin had him stand on a chair while we all passed by and put our hand on his heart to know how dangerously fast it was beating because of the stressful exercise he had just undergone. I do not know whatever happened to this boy, but I always wondered how badly his psyche might have been scarred as a result of having to stand on that chair.

Third grade was also memorable because I encountered a really mean teacher who, I'm convinced, really hated kids. Interestingly, she was the only teacher I had who lived outside the district. Yes, we learned the curriculum, but when we did something wrong in the classroom, we were belittled. Talkers had to wear horse collars made out of construction paper, and God help those poor souls who crinkled or tore the collars. This action was typical of this woman's bullying, and she got in really serious trouble one day when a very upset little girl in her class left school and walked for miles along a very busy road to reach home. The woman left the school district

9

shortly after, and the girl survived unscathed and unscarred. It was not a happy year.

Springtown School was a pleasant change. Our teacher taught both fourth and fifth grades, and so she split the time equally between both groups. There was no central heat in the building, and each room was fired by a woodstove. Periodically, a boy would be sent to the basement for firewood, and the teacher would stoke the fire. Irregularly, a farmer would show up with a load of firewood, and some boys would go help him unload his Model A Ford truck. Even then, it seemed old. Behind the school was a large pile of ashes, which we watered down in the winter so we could slide down it during recesses. When the weather was nice, we played baseball, kickball, or whatever other game someone dreamed up. We learned how to create our own fun. At lunch we were allowed to toast the sandwiches we had brought from home. There was a definite homey atmosphere to the room and the learning activities. We began each day with a Bible reading, the recitation of the Lord's Prayer, and the Pledge of Allegiance to the flag. We had both fire and bomb drills regularly. How anyone thought we would survive an atomic bomb blast while sitting on the floor with our heads bowed and our hands crossed over our necks is beyond me. The curriculum and teaching methods continued to be standard fare of the time, but there was clearly an awareness by the two teachers of Springtown School that world events were important. In January 1953, President Eisenhower was inaugurated. At that time, there were few television sets in Springtown, but on that day, the teachers had us walk from the school to homes where there were TVs. We watched the inauguration. Then we walked back to school, discussed the event, and climbed on the buses to go home.

Halfway through grade five, we left Springtown School, which closed, and went to Pleasant Valley. The move was the result of the merger, and we were joined by students from Zion Hill and Passer. We all went to the old high school, which seemed massive after Springtown School. We did all the late-elementary school stuff, but on a bigger scale than we were used to. I do remember that some of the kids living in Pleasant Valley went home for lunch. The rest of us brought ours. One day I forgot mine, and a kind classmate took me to his house so I wouldn't starve. The sense of community came early to us. Most schools had safety patrols, students used to help others on the school buses or crosswalks. At the end of the school year, we were taken to a major-league ball game as a reward for our diligence of duty. On the given day, we climbed on a school bus and went to Philadelphia to watch the Philadelphia As, later the Kansas City and then Oakland As, play an afternoon game. That trip was absolute magic to those of us totally enamored with baseball. Of course, we all were. Sixth grade the following year was the logical extension of fifth with a different teacher. At the end of that year, we all went to the new high school, where life became very different.

I think my elementary school experience was pretty typical of rural schooling in that decade. America had just experienced the Great Depression and World War II. Most of the citizens of the communities had pretty similar roots with similar value systems. There was a pecking order in the local society, which was respected by most. Curriculum and teaching methods, which were very dull by today's standards, had not been altered drastically over the past fifty years, but the educational process was about to make some giant changes. Nor do I think the academic demands were particularly demanding. There were no state-mandated end-of-the-year tests, and promotion decisions were made by teachers who developed their own measurements. Most of the elementary teachers were women who had taught for a long while, and they pushed concepts important to their communities: religion, patriotism, learning skills, and proper social behavior. They worked hard at their task and felt kinship with their students, who were the children of their neighbors and friends. Classes were large with students of varying ability levels, but there was no such thing as special education or advanced classes for the best and the brightest. In lots of schools, there was no principal, and teachers handled their own problems. There were relatively few discipline problems largely because we knew we would get punished severely at home if we were in trouble at school. The values of the community found their way into the school and were instilled within the students. Education was then a much-easier process than it has now become.

The 1950s: Land of Ozzie and Harriet

Paradise High School was a vastly different place from Pleasant Valley School. First, it was new and pretty. Second, it housed students from grades seven to twelve; thus, there were many bodies of all different sizes there. Third, none of us knew a majority of the students. Fourth, we knew even fewer of the teachers. Finally, we were the youngest kids in the school. There was much to learn.

The Paradise School District came about in the late 1940s, when five small school districts realized they had neither the facilities nor revenue to continue operating individually. The facilities were outdated (many one-room schools), and the postwar population was growing incredibly fast. The merger allowed for a modern high school that could offer a full range of curriculum. This process of school district consolidation was going on all over the country, and while it created wonderful new opportunities, it also presented problems, many of which would continue through the rest of the century. This combining activity was really the beginning of all sorts of educational and societal experimentations and movements. In many ways, it was the beginning of the "bigger is better" mantra that would turn into "it's too big to fail" mentality. But in the early 1950s in our corner of the world, the creation of this new school district brought a wonderful new high school that housed grades seven to twelve.

We met different kids, changed classes, and faced new challenges. As in any school, there was a mix of teachers: some good, some bad, and most pretty mediocre. They worked hard at trying to teach us as our hormones raged, and they did pretty well, considering that a majority of the students then turned out to be good people with decent careers. In retrospect, I think there was not an air of great expectations for student achievement. Teachers followed prescribed lesson plans with little thought or vigor. Too much class time was spent on meaningless drills or other time fillers. Students were rarely asked to use and develop creative-thinking skills. As long as students were orderly and pleasant, all was well with the teachers. For example, I do not remember writing one essay or report during my middle school years. That lack would haunt me later. Only a few teachers pushed students hard, and because the district was new, there was not a history of academic achievement. I can remember being bored most of the time and getting in trouble as a result. Because little was demanded of me, I did little and developed no good study habits. Upon reflection, I realize that without academic demand, I had no sense of academic achievement and what it should bring. Instead, I figured out ways to skip classes and torment teachers. Only a few good ones knew their stuff and demanded as they should have. Mr. Hand, who taught math, and Mrs. Gackenbach, who taught Latin and German, stand out as those teachers who pushed.

Mr. Hand taught algebra with an iron fist. He demanded our understanding of the concepts and accepted no less than perfection from us. Yet underneath his grim exterior was the patience of Job in teaching those of us finding algebraic concepts to come from another planet. What became clear to us all was that he loved and respected algebra, but he liked and respected us as well. Furthermore, anyone having Mr. Hand in class will remember his famous saying, especially when one was trying to fudge on homework: "You can fool some of the people all of the time, and you can fool all of the people some of the time, but you can't fool all of the people all of the time." He also had a great grin whenever he allowed it to sneak out. His seriousness of purpose and his kindness showed through. He was a great teacher with a huge wow factor.

Mrs. Gackenbach taught Latin and German with firmness equal to that of Mr. Hand. There was no random seating in her class. A student's seat was determined by the grade on the latest test. Those of us who did not fare well got to sit in the front row. While there were seating changes regularly, some of us never seemed to escape the hated front row. There was no hiding in the back for those who wanted to. Rightfully believing that the educational process involved parents as well as students and teachers, she sent our poor test grades home to be signed by parents, thus ensuring their knowledge of our academic shortcomings. Explaining unacceptable grades was not fun at my house. While Mrs. Gackenbach ruled with an iron fist, she also had a heart of gold, and she loved her students. She took many on trips to Europe, and there was a steady stream of kids through her house. She was respected and loved by her students.

Mr. Mann, the only art teacher, in a quiet way asked for and received excellent student work. Art was fun because the assignments were creative and interesting. While we struggled with projects, this nice man directed and supported our efforts. As a result, we saw tangible, positive results. Mr. Mann was laid back, yet he, too, expected decent effort and results. He produced some students who went on to become art teachers and professional artists, thus speaking well for his aegis. It was clear to us that he liked and respected students even when we were not at our best.

There were some really weak teachers who created instant boredom, which resulted in classroom mayhem. Ms. Failure comes to mind. We have all had teachers we despised because of their incompetence. Ms. Failure was one. She taught Pennsylvania History to ninth graders, not an easy task. Close to retirement age and devoid of passion, skill, and discipline, she let people in the class run over her. She clearly had no respect for us. Instead, I think, she feared us, and some of us worked hard to make her life miserable. We were remarkably successful, and every class was a fight between her and us. We played all sorts of tricks on her, and no one had any respect for her at all. In a sense she wasted taxpayers' money by being in that classroom, and I doubt any of us remembers any worthwhile fact of Pennsylvania history from that class. Her energy was gone. So was her will to teach. She just had to hang in there for another year or two to gain her retirement package, and time spent in her class was a total loss to her students. I use her simply as an illustration of a worn-out pedagogue caught in the economic system. We abused her and lessened ourselves in the process.

If anything, this problem of worn-out teachers has grown worse across the land. Now we are faced with the coming retirement of the baby boomers, an economic problem to be sure but quite probably a benefit to the students in the classroom. Most of these people are tired and beaten down. The students are increasingly becoming unruly, and the courts and society have caused school administrators not to support their teachers. As a result, many have given up trying to pursue excellence in the classroom and just hang on to survive. They also face the degradation of having legislators, in their quest to reduce costs, suggest that teacher salaries, pensions, and benefits are places to cut costs in budgets. In a sense, the legislators are looking for ways to break promises to people who have worked hard at nonprincely incomes for the good of the public. As a result, there is a growing cynicism and fear among our teachers. Furthermore, because of current teaching situations, good college students do not look toward teaching as a viable career. We have to change national mind-sets about teachers and teaching.

Going back to the Paradise School system, we have another good man to examine. Mr. Brown was the principal, and he was a thoroughly nice man. He, too, was at the end of his career, and I think he basically hoped the school would get through each day without a disaster. It did in most cases largely because the kids were well behaved and docile as a bunch. Mr. Brown took his afternoon stroll through the building at the time when I was in Ms. Failure's class. Her room was very close to the main office door, and when Mr. Brown entered the hall, he frequently saw me standing outside the door to my class. He would sigh, walk down to where I was, and ask whether I was still out or out again. He told me once that I should be a teacher because I knew every trick in the book. Maybe he did help me toward my profession. He was kind, and he knew what the problem was in that room. He chose to let nature take its course rather than create a big stir. He knew he was stuck with Ms. Failure until she retired and that we would pass on to other teachers, leaving her alone.

I do not remember other teachers by name, a fact that leads me to understand that they had no impact on me. Hopefully, they had greater effect on some of my classmates. My sense is that we did too much drill work in class rather than creative problem solving and that the community accepted such activity without much question. People were tired of conflict then. We had just gone through World War II and the Korean Conflict, and people were more interested in cashing in on a growing economy than questioning educational processes. In any case, my parents were not happy with my academic progress, and they forced me to attend a different kind of school.

Coming from a weak school district, I was not prepared for what I faced at the very good boarding school I attended for high school. Most of my classmates had come from excellent elementary and middle schools in the New York, Philadelphia, Chicago, and other wealthy suburbs. As a result, this high school's curriculum took into consideration their preparation and the need to place its students in the finest colleges in the land. Within three weeks, I was in serious academic trouble because I was behind in every class. I had already failed two English essays. It was apparent that I needed to repeat Latin 1 rather than continue in Latin 2 simply because the students in this school had covered twice as much material in Latin 1 than I had, and I was in dire straits. My experience in Algebra 2 was almost as bad, and the only way I survived was being tutored during vacations by Mr. Hand. By Thanksgiving break, my academic confidence had totally disappeared, and socially, I was just as lost. The drill instructors at Parris Island could not have broken me down more. It took three years to regain a sense of worth. My lack of success, loneliness, and homesickness made me a miserable being, yet I knew to put on my happy face around my parents during vacations. That was hard to do when report cards came in and my mother expressed her feelings about my various shortcomings.

Fortunately, I encountered a few teachers who set me on the right path, and I came to realize what a good school this one was. Mr. Hall, the head, set the tone. He demanded effort from his staff and his students. Those who disobeyed rules disappeared, and the community was told why. While I did not like him as a person, I respected the quality of the school he ran. I was just beginning to understand that the clientele of the institution demanded excellence on all fronts. He understood that demand and catered to it. As a result, students were pushed in every area of school life. We had classes and mandatory athletics six days a week, and we attended chapel daily. Fun is not an idea that crosses my mind when I think of the place. Survival is, and I got through the experience and found a college willing to accept me. Mr. Hall impressed me to the point that I knew that someday I wanted to work at a good school.

The man I really owe most thanks to is Mr. Asals. He taught me how to write, and the task was not easy. After I had miserably failed a couple of essays, Mr. Asals invited me to some tutoring sessions. He was a very young teacher who lived on a dormitory floor, where he was responsible for the safety and well-being of some twenty students. I shall never forget going down that dreary hall, knocking at his door, and entering the room, which was no larger than twelve feet by fifteen feet. All the woodwork in the room was grim, dark Victorian brown, and the only furniture was an iron bed, a student desk, two wooden chairs, and a beat-up dresser. A single bulb, no larger than 60 watts, hung from a cord in the center of the ceiling, and a gooseneck lamp with a smaller bulb sat on the desk. Mr. Asals' bathrobe and pajamas hung from a hook on the inside of the door. The setting came right out of a grim gothic novel. This nice man would greet me with a sigh, and we would sit at the desk. He would then pull out my latest essay and go over it word by word and punctuation mark by punctuation mark. At first I had no clue as to what he said, but I began to get inklings. By the end of the year, I could write competent but not good essays. He led me to the light at the end of the tunnel.

Years later, I realized what a tremendous influence he had on me. Many of my teaching methods are based on those he displayed to me. While he demanded good performance, he treated me, and other students, with respect and kindness. He understood that each of us was important, and he went about his tasks accordingly. I grew under his tutelage. Other teachers and lots of experience helped hone my writing skills, but I owe him more than I can ever pay.

One other teacher there needs to be mentioned only because of the force of his personality. Mr. Whitely taught biology, a class which met after lunch. He was a rather zany character who, among other things, loved to sail. I think he had a place on the water somewhere in Massachusetts or Maine. He always wore a white lab coat, and his hair, a little too long, appeared to be always unruly. His means of presentation bordered on the theatrical, and as a result, his classes were fun. I shall never forget the spring day when he sensed our total inattention to his words of wisdom. Suddenly he disappeared into the lab behind his classroom and reappeared with a hidden firecracker that exploded in the sink before him. He got our undivided attention for the rest of the class. Talk about wow factor.

Life at that school was demanding, and I grew as a result of my attendance there. The teachers were, on the most part, kind professionals who taught their subjects well. Maybe it was the era, but many of those instructors spent their whole careers there, retiring only after teaching generations of students. One unmarried man, unhappy at his coming retirement, saw fit to die quietly in his bathtub after consuming too many martinis. He couldn't face the outside world. Even at a school of such quality, there were some teachers who were less than good. They were weeded out over time and replaced by others who, hopefully, were better. The demand for excellence was readily apparent throughout the program, and all, faculty and students, were held to it.

My experience at this school convinced me that students should face realistic but tough demands in the classroom. As I look back at the time I spent in the Paradise School District, I realize we were not pushed hard enough, and thus, we did not learn to expect only the best from ourselves. Without goals, there is no incentive or means to learn. Skills become polished only when they are practiced, and intellectual horizons are broadened only when we have to reach. Compromise of goals is not a positive force in the educational process. For example, children operate best when they know their limits and the consequences if they do not live up to them. The military takes kids from all walks of life and makes good soldiers and sailors out of them by demanding that the recruits live up to the standards demanded of them. We teachers owe it to our students to show them the demands and help them reach the goals. For best results, we must do so with fairness, firmness, and kindness. We can never forget that **each student** is the most important person in the room, and it is our obligation to have each leave our classroom a person of better skills and broader horizons.

The 1960s: The Decade of Chaos

For me the decade began with my graduation from high school and matriculation into Washington and Jefferson College. It was then a good, small, all-male school in western Pennsylvania, and it has since become a far better coed college with about twice as many students. On May 8, 1960, I had never heard of it. On May 11, I applied at the suggestion of a kind man who knew what he was doing. On May 19, I was accepted, and the following day I sent the required check. I saw the place for the first time at the end of June after I was committed to attend. I did not make a mistake.

W&J was just the right place for me. It was small, and there were good teachers and good guys from all walks of life. I became a fully engaged student in a short time, and because of good preparation at my high school and a determination on my part to do well, I did just that. On the whole, the faculty was experienced and talented. Many were as funny as they were demanding, and they wanted us to succeed. Of course, some students did not, but most did and became very successful in their various professions.

I think one of the most positive aspects of my collegiate experience was the close bonding that took place during those four years. As a result, many of us still keep close contact after leaving there close to fifty years ago. Over the years, our families also have become a part of the W&J family, bringing a broadening of friendship and interest among one another. This closeness is a result of the school's being small. We knew and liked one another. Certainly, the college, directly or indirectly, taught us a sense of community.

Yes, there were teachers who stood out, whom we still talk about all these years later. Without a doubt, they impressed us with their wisdom, knowledge, and strong personalities. Some did so quietly, others loudly. Either way, the good ones ruled.

Dr. Mitchell taught English history. An older man close to retirement, he taught his subject by telling wonderful stories and made the English monarchs come alive. The only problem with his class was that he spoke so quietly that students would run for the close seats and latecomers would push closer and closer. Occasionally, Dr. Mitchell would complain, and everyone would back off just a little bit. Most of us took him for several courses happily, and we worked hard to do well.

Dr. Branton, a professor of English, flat blew me away. He loved the Victorian era of English literature, and I really think he was a Victorian at heart. He was a crisp, small man who could be overlooked easily in a crowd but not in a classroom. One semester, he taught a course on Victorian poetry, which I took. He liked to read the poetry to bring it alive. One day in class, I looked up just as we turned a page. He did not, but he continued reciting the poem without looking at the book. I began to watch him, and he never turned the page. The poetry was in his head. He never misread. Never had I encountered a memory like his, and I began to spend more than a little bit of time in his office. He had received his PhD from Harvard with a concentration in English poetry. He told me that part of his doctoral exam was to identify 200 spot quotations from English poetry. He said that he had identified correctly 196. He had found three others later, and he insisted that the faculty had made one up. His knowledge just overwhelmed me.

He was not without humor. In another course from him—this one about Victorian novels—I had written a term paper about William Makepeace Thackeray, a prominent novelist of the era. When I got it back, I noticed only one very short comment on the cover. It said, "How stupid can you get?" Puzzled, I looked at him. He looked back and just shook his head. Again I looked at my paper only to realize that I had misspelled Thackeray consistently throughout the paper. He had a point. We became very good friends and corresponded for many years after I had gone on to my own teaching career.

There was a campus character nicknamed Screaming Tony. He taught Spanish and Latin American history. His main means of instruction was intimidation, and he had a strong following of students willing to put up with his abuse and learn the given subject. Certainly, he was a campus character, and I suspect his bark was worse than his bite, but one semester was enough for me. He was correct in demanding good performance from his students because learning academic rigor is a significant part of a college education, but he demeaned and belittled students in the process. I have always thought one can teach more effectively with kindness rather than vitriol.

Paul Reardon was a prince of a man. He was the director of athletics and the swimming coach. I spent four years swimming for him, and he taught me as much about myself as did anyone else.

Although he was in his mid-fifties when I knew him, he still could beat any swimmer on the team in any stroke for one length of the pool. He taught me to be tougher and more demanding on myself, and he did it with hard work and kindness. He treated us all like sons. He liked and respected those who worked hard for him, and we did all we could for him. He taught decency, and he taught it by example. For thirty years after my graduation, I found ways to either see or talk to him. I miss him now that he has gone.

I remember a philosophy professor who was one of the strangest men on campus. But then maybe philosophy teachers are supposed to be strange. Anyway, at the beginning of each class, he would take an unfiltered cigarette from his pocket and tap it on his lighter for better than half the class. Then he would smoke it. As soon as he finished, he would reach in another pocket and pull a Kool cigarette from the pack and commence packing it. He drove us nuts doing that, and I'm sure he did so deliberately. I often wondered whether his actions were deliberate or instinctual, but they certainly distracted us from philosophical points. His personality dominated the class, but I wonder to what end. To me he was an example of a teacher whose actions got in the way of what he was trying to accomplish. Maybe that was just the philosopher in him speaking at depths I failed to understand. He did like fraternity parties and was a regular visitor at ours.

The finest teacher I ever had was Dr. Porter. He and his colleague Dr. Dieter built a premed program that was second to none. When we were students, anyone completing that program was guaranteed admission to med school. All students in the college were required to take a lab science course, and most of us nonscientific types took Dr. Porter's botany class. He made it perfectly clear in the first meeting what his expectations were and what would happen if we failed to meet them. As a result, we worked extremely hard in his class and did very well, which was what he wanted. We never cut labs, which unfortunately was for three hours on Friday afternoons, or classes, some of which met on Saturday morning. To miss was a major sin. Dr. Porter began his class the minute he was supposed to, and he hated tardiness. If a student was foolhardy enough to enter the room late, Dr. Porter would pause in his lecture until the unfortunate soul sat down, and then he would proceed to ask that student a barrage of questions about the material discussed in his absence. One was not late a second time. But he was a man of immense humor, and he knew when to throw jokes into his lectures. Most of his jests were pure corn, but they came when we were drifting off. On one Saturday morning of a party weekend, Dr. Porter was halfway through a lecture when the door opened and an obviously very hung-over student stumbled in. Dr. Porter stopped his lecture, watched the culprit seek a chair, and quipped, "Someone pull down the sheets for McSwain." We all howled with pure joy. Then back to botany we went. Dr. Porter was a craftsman in the field of teaching, and we appreciated him.

There were many other very competent teachers there, and students were well prepared for the graduate work that most of us went on to do. There is little doubt that every student at W&J of my era could name at least one professor who was memorable to him. Excellent teaching was the signature of the place when we attended, and it still is. It is fitting that the college has continued to serve students well through the turbulent times we have lived through. I am convinced that it and the students it now serves are stronger than it and we were fifty years ago. While the college is built on solid traditional values and means of instruction, it has adopted the methods of technology to provide students with even stronger and more diverse learning experiences. Most importantly, high-quality instruction remains the core upon which all else at the college is built.

At some point in college, I decided that I wanted to teach in the independent school world. Even though I had not found my experience there to be a happy one, I respected the quality of the education provided. Teachers in that world did not then have to gain state certification. In most cases, they scoffed at it, feeling that they were above such mundane criteria. Hence, I took no education courses at W&J. I was to regret that decision later. In 1964 I was graduated from college to enter a rapidly changing world.

The 1960s began quietly, but a major change took place almost immediately. The then eldest president in our history, Dwight D. Eisenhower, gave way to the youngest, John F. Kennedy. We young people were ecstatic because we really felt in touch with the youth movement in Washington. Mr. and Mrs. Kennedy brought a glamor to the head of our land that had been missing for a long time. A child, John-John, was born during this term, and life seemed to be picking up its pace. Then President Kennedy was assassinated, bringing a pall to the land. He was replaced by another old-timer, Lyndon Johnson, and the young again felt left out of power. We mourned the death of our president and the loss of his Camelot, and we began to experience other factors that would tear our country's value system to pieces. The

Cold War heated up into a really nasty war over Vietnam, where far too many of our generation lost their lives. The civil rights movement, which had its beginnings in the previous decades, tore our country apart. Furthermore, television brought the horrors of both conflicts into our homes nightly, intensifying the angst. Drugs hit mainstream America. Rock and roll developed into protest music, and hard and then acid rock angered our parents' generation. Marches of all sorts dominated Washington, DC, and there were more assassinations of popular, important political figures. Gone were Martin Luther King Jr., Malcolm X, and Robert Kennedy. Students had sit-ins in universities, protesting all sorts of issues. Riots broke out in Watts, Detroit, and Washington, DC. Families got torn apart over Vietnam, drugs, and free love.

By the end of the decade, chaos was rampant, and violence common. Yet our institutions, while tested, rallied and held. The planned government of our founding fathers withstood all sorts of pressures. Life had changed, and not all for the better. We moved toward an era where people of all races and religions are legally recognized as having equal rights. The effects of the traumatic actions of this decade are felt yet today, and the issues have not been put to bed. Yet we handle them differently, and better than we did then.

School systems were attacked by issues coming from the national pressures. Integration, which had begun in Arkansas, caused major upheavals of schools. So did continued consolidation of smaller districts. Both changes made it more difficult for individuals to sense that the schoolhouse was the focal point of the community because the growth of the district made the entity more impersonal. At the same time, there was a change of direction in curriculum. The space race dominated school policy because of the increased need for engineers and scientists. America was behind in the race and had to not only catch up but surpass. A greater push toward having all students take college preparatory programs left a void for students who either did not want to go or who were not capable of going to college. As a result, many students did not do well in school and suffered from declining self-esteem. We forgot in this space race that people in all walks of life are important to the smooth running of our society.

Major experimentation of curriculum began. Greater use of technology began to change curriculum delivery. Studies about different learning processes began to appear, and focus on individualized learning began. In a quest for better learning and cost efficiency, some schools moved toward large group–small group instruction. The result was that while many new strategies were tried, people lost focus on the outcomes. Experimentation was cool, but did it really improve the education of the child? I wonder sometimes if at that point greater reliance on technological advances resulted more in entertaining than in teaching. Time would tell. The combination of pressures of continued growth within school districts and demand for academic change took their toll.

The mass media didn't help the schools either. The news seemed to find problems in schools and harp on them almost nightly. Ugly integration issues found their way into America's living rooms daily. As the media focused on the various difficulties in society, it heightened the growing disregard for institutions and laws. High school students watched their counterparts in college hold sit-ins in administrative offices. They saw how disruptions made the news. Their own disregard for law and order began to grow, and they felt a need to express their discontent. The arts and media also showed us regularly that our mores were out of date. Free love was in. So was wild dress. So was an unkempt lifestyle that lured the young away from the older, more puritanical ethic we had known and practiced. Life was changing fast, and schools had to adapt to the changes. The process was not easy or well accepted in communities. Life then was a ride on a wild roller coaster. Emotions and rants ruled rather than logic. Our schools were not a place for the weak and weary.

As the decade progressed, so too did the use of drugs of all sorts. The effects on some, particularly the hallucinogens, were devastating to many. The violence that came with the drug culture tore schools and communities apart. At a lesser level, the laid-back attitude heightened by lesser drugs affected student performance and academic drive negatively. Stoned students just went through the day in a stupor. Unfortunately, this problem lives with us today but in a different way. And it's not likely to go away soon.

Amid the gathering clouds of national unrest, I went to work for a long established boarding school in Pennsylvania. In existence for more than one hundred years, it embodied a traditional prep school life. The academic program was, and still is, college preparatory, and the campus life worked to develop well-rounded graduates well on the way to becoming leaders in our communities. Athletics was a dominant feature of the program, and all students had to participate on teams two out of the three terms of the school year. Spiritual well-being dominated the program with regular chapel sessions. Graduates went on to fine colleges and universities.

New faculty members walked into a tradition with strong mentors working diligently to produce good products. Each month we had full faculty meetings to discuss campus issues and programs. We had regular department meetings focusing on building strong curriculum and delivery. We sought consistency of academic excellence by developing departmental exams for courses and continually evaluating the materials used. We argued about teaching methods and were led by mentors who really cared. Twice a year we had faculty meetings to discuss the progress of every student in the school. The sessions and recommendations were very serious. For example, when discussing a student with academic or behavioral problems, we sometimes suggested removal from school. Always, the best interest of the student was at the forefront of the discussion. We cared about and nurtured students. This training helped most new faculty become strong teachers as it focused on the most important people in the school: the student.

One other aspect about the school we learned quickly. We were expected to give our lives to the school during the academic year. In the English Department, those of us carrying a full load had five classes with two preparations. Typically, we assigned forty pages of reading a night per class and a five-hundred-word essay each week. We also assigned a term paper at least twice a year. Because this was a boarding school, we monitored dormitory floors at night, coached teams, supervised other activities, and prepared for class. The days were long. At the same time, many of us married and had children, and so we were learning to balance workload with family demands. My wife could not get over the constant mountain of papers I had to read. The experienced staff led by example because they worked just as hard, or harder, than we did. The young staff members learned to work smart as well as hard, and we took that lesson with us when we left. I suspect that similar pressures befell teachers at all schools the same way. Many of our wives taught in the local public systems, and they had as much work to do as we, and they were just as dedicated.

Very interesting currents began to affect the school. First, there was a big faculty turnover. Many long-term teachers retired. Others went to greener pastures. Financial pressures on the school caused the administration to select more first—and second-year teachers than they had been used to. That factor had an adverse impact on the instructional program as it would have had anywhere. As the decade progressed, many of the young instructors came to the school only for the reason of avoiding the war in Vietnam. Rebellious in nature, many not only did not buy into the established practices of the school, but they also sought to subvert them. Others were totally caught up in the currents outside the school and sympathetic with many of them. Their attendance in marches on Washington caused controversy in our institution. The unity of the faculty took a major hit, and the students, all hyped up in their own spirit of rebellion, worked to use the divide to their advantage. This rebellion climaxed on campus when the student body walked out of chapel one morning as the head of school spoke. A very spiritual man, the head was appalled, and later that day submitted his resignation to the board of trustees. They did not accept it, and he remained head for another several years, but his spirit was broken. He did not deserve this fate.

And then there were drugs. We began to see more and more signs of them. Attitudes and behavior changed among more of the students. Performance in the classroom began to slip, and most on the faculty and administration had little concept of how to confront and handle this problem. Few people in America did for that matter. But the school tried. It held seminars and debates on the subject. In fact, Timothy Leary, the chief guru of the LSD movement, appeared on our stage to debate a doctor from MIT on the impact of drugs on people. Many of us thought Leary shot himself in the foot by being so high that he was virtually incoherent. But the students, being full-blown teenagers, were not convinced of the evils of drugs. Nor are some today. In any case, we faced the same drug-related issues that virtually every school system in the country was facing, and we dealt with them in the best way we could. I think it's safe to say that a strong majority of our students came out of the experience without major harm.

In the late '60s, there was strong student fear and anger over Vietnam. Kids knew that they had to get good grades to get into college, and if they failed to do so, they would wind up fighting in the jungles, where they might likely die. Any poor or mediocre grade was fought by a student. They were convinced that we the teachers were out to send them to war by giving poor grades. Self-blame for poor performance did not exist. So frequently, a class became a battleground. Fortunately for all of us, virtually every student at that school went on to college and did well, but the tensions were high every day in the classroom trenches.

One eleventh-grade English class I taught in 1968 illustrated this issue, but not without humor. It met right before lunch, and every discussion seemed difficult and intense. Students attacked with vehemence any point made in discussion. In the class was one student not known for his academic prowess, and every day with about twenty minutes to go, he'd raise his hand and ask, "What's for lunch?" The class would groan. One day we were talking about a particular poem, and Bill raised his hand. Instead of asking his usual question, he said that he really liked the poem. In total surprise, the class roared in laughter, and that day we all went to lunch a unified, happy bunch. But that was a rare occurrence. I think I learned more about teaching in that class alone than I did anywhere else. The group made me work very hard to justify every comment, test question, and maybe my own existence as a teacher. I am in a way indebted to that group as it made me realize that the progress of each student is the most important issue in any classroom.

This school was committed to the training of its faculty as well as that of its students. Many of us earned our master's degrees at the expense of the school. In return, we agreed to remain on the faculty for at least two years after receiving our degree. Certainly, that demand was fair, and the school benefitted from our advanced knowledge. I went to Lehigh University for three summers and wrote my thesis during the following school year. My last exam took place the day after our men landed on the moon for the first time. Needless to say, I did not cram as well as I should have but did well on the exam anyway.

The English faculty at Lehigh was distinguished when I attended, and the workload was incredible. As in the case of any faculty, there were characters. One man had a running fight with the lawn-mowing arm of the grounds crew, and both sides enjoyed the battle. Lawn mowers invaded the grounds right outside our classroom regularly during this man's class. He would roar outside, do battle with the operator, who might or might not leave. As a result, our man would return either as cocky as a bantam rooster or vanquished. In any case, we enjoyed the break from his lecture. Another professor regularly taught Shakespeare to classes of two hundred students or more. The summer we joined forces, there were about twelve students. The professor sat in his chair, put his feet on the desk, and talked Shakespeare. There was lots of give and take during the session, and we all enjoyed it. The Chaucer specialist was very near retirement and very formal with little humor. His class was all business, and no one dared to be a slacker. All these professors were accomplished in their fields, and their sheer knowledge was incredible. We went to class for several hours per day and then spent endless additional hours in the stacks of the library, reading dusty journals and tomes. I took a Chaucer class, and we read a tale a day and were responsible for citing every journal article ever written about a certain area affecting the tale. For instance, someone in the class had the area of battle between the sexes. Now when we read "The Wife of Bath's Tale," that poor soul had hundreds of articles to find. We all took our turns in academic purgatory when the professor would quietly ask, "And what did so-and-so have to say on this point?" One summer I had two courses: one on contemporary British novels and one on Shakespearian drama. We read a novel or two a week and a play a class. I rarely finished reading before midnight. The pace was incredible, but we were exposed to vast amounts of literature and scholarly research. Those summers were tough, but with regular class time, I had the will and need to prepare daily. Suddenly, I knew what serious academic work was, and that discovery made me a better teacher.

The thesis was another matter. I knew myself well enough to understand that I had to devote a regular time block during the week to the thesis. Without doing so, I would never get it written. Fortunately, several of my colleagues were studying at a local state university. I rode to that campus with them, and while they were in class, I went to the library and did the research and writing necessary. The strategy worked, and in June 1970, I received my MA in English.

In the very late '60s, I also had a chance to experience a national testing program from a perspective not seen by many. About 1967, the SAT included a writing sample. I was one of four hundred readers used to evaluate those samples. The readers came from all fifty states. Half were from secondary schools and half from college staffs. We met in Atlantic City, New Jersey (before it was refurbished), over a long weekend and read student essays by the thousands. We were grouped in tables of eight to read. Initially, we read samples to be trained toward evaluating fairly and consistently. Each essay was given a score from 1 to 4, and each was read by at least three readers. Believe me, we earned the stipends we were paid, and by the time we got home, we did not want to read anything for a while.

The experience was enlightening in that we gained a better understanding of what was expected in those essays. We could then take that knowledge back to our schools and improve the preparation for the next several classes to improve their scores on the test. We also gained a better sense that our school sampling of the scores was a very small segment of the whole. The knowledge was sort of like learning that Coca-Cola sells millions of Cokes per minute. It made us feel pretty small, yet at the same time, we felt pretty special for working on a national project. The experience caused us to understand more fully the need to keep our academic standards high and to push our students. Suddenly, we saw that college admissions was indeed a national contest at the finest colleges and universities, and our students needed to be prepared properly to compete favorably.

All these factors affected us as people and as teachers. We had to defend the values we lived by. One we held was the need for academic rigor. Our students were headed to very good colleges, and they had to be prepared properly. We did not let up on our demands, and the students responded with the required effort. Sometimes in the defense of values, we had to examine them diligently and decide whether or not they were worth holding. We had to learn new techniques to deal positively with students. We had to hang on in the maelstrom of the '60s and adapt daily to wild behavioral swings in students. Most of us became better teachers in the process.

We cannot leave a discussion of this decade without commenting on a major miracle that happened during it. In 1961, President Kennedy vowed that we would put a man on the moon. The Russians had beaten us into space, and our national leader was determined to have us win the space race. In 1969, we put the first man on the moon. In the process, schools and universities totally revamped and improved math and science curricula. There was a national mandate for the improvement. In many ways the whole world changed in the decade of the space race. Millions of kids became interested in engineering and science careers, and scientific knowledge exploded. This phenomenon had to be one of the glorious highs of the decade.

Nor can we forget that most kids growing up in schools during this decade behaved themselves, went to school, and became fine people and citizens in an increasingly tough world. These results came because most parents and teachers did good jobs raising and developing the youngsters moving toward adulthood.

The 1970s: A Period of Growth

I accepted the position of head of the English Department at a small independent day school in Charlotte, North Carolina, for the fall of 1970. I loved North Carolina the moment I arrived, and forty-two years later, I still do. In many ways this decade was one of growth and experimentation for me and for the city and country as well.

In 1970, the population of Charlotte was less than half of what it is today. The school district had nine high schools, and the whole district underwent a major change that year. The US federal court mandated that each school in the system must have the same racial mixture as did the city at that point. As a result, thousands of students, both black and white, were bused across town to achieve that new standard. While no one liked the situation, people in Charlotte handled it with dignity. There were no riots or uprisings. Instead, there was an air of determination to make this new plan work. There were some administrative issues, especially student assignment, but in about three years, the plan that worked for nearly twenty-five years was in place. Other cities, particularly Boston, faced the same federal pressure about the same time, and they handled it with anger and strife, almost in direct defiance with the federal law. In Charlotte there was no defiance. In fact, there was just the opposite. Families from all neighborhoods worked together to make schools the best possible learning environment possible for all children. The citizens rose to the occasion and made the best of a situation they did not like.

Maybe the peaceful schools helped serve as an impetus to the rapid growth of Charlotte over the next two decades. In any case, the city changed dramatically, and the school system grew exponentially. All these rapid changes in the school world also brought about tremendous growth of independent schools in the Charlotte area. In 1970 alone, two new independent schools and many church-sponsored schools began life. Unquestionably, there was some white flight from the public system, but there was also increased demand for independent education caused by influx of people from other parts of the country where this option was readily available. That demand continues forty years later, and as a result, there are many more charter, independent and church-supported schools available.

This decade was one of growth, especially of big organizations. Consolidated school districts grew at unprecedented paces, major corporations swallowed up smaller companies, and unheard-of names such as WalMart became household and then dominant words in our vocabulary. Small businesses faced tougher and tougher competition from the giant corporations, and the groundwork was laid for the problems we had later with the multinational corporations changing our way of life completely. We were to learn that bigger is not always better, especially when the bigger, international corporations took jobs away from this country and increased dependence on technological advances increased productivity at the cost of even more jobs. The bigger institutions became, the less responsive they were to individuals.

Another societal change was taking place in the schools. Back in the 1940s, the GI Bill opened college doors for many people who never had any hope or aspirations for college. Secondary schools pushed college prep courses for all students, ignoring the needs of a major portion of our population. The message across the land was clear: go to college or be a nobody. Valuable programs designed to teach people skills in manufacturing facilities, farms, and necessary service industries took backseats, and the students in them were looked upon as lesser beings headed to dead-end jobs. We made a mistake.

All over this country, standards continued to slip. Certainly, quality of manufacturing did as seen particularly in the auto industry. Toyotas, Volkswagens, etc., became big sellers here because they were better built, and our sleeping auto industry let the change happen. In schools, academic standards and performance slipped. For example, in 1970, the average US SAT score was 1,039, and in 1979, it fell to 908, a drop of 131 points (www.satscores.us.faq/what-is-the—average sat-score.asp). The College Board and the educational bureaucracy have published many justifications that the scores slipped badly because there was a much larger number of students taking the test, thus diluting the scores. While there is truth to that point, underlying it is the fact that a majority of those students taking the SAT in that span were and had been studying in American schools where the job was not being done very well by parents, teachers, and administrators (*The SAT: Four Major Modifications of the 1970–85 Era* by John R. Valley, College Board report no. 92–1). We became too proud of our fancy new school consolidations and did not look closely enough at the performances in them. We felt invincible.

It would be totally unfair to ignore the melting-pot quality of our nation when looking at this issue. True, immigration brought many new people from all over the world, creating difficulties in the classroom. Yet certain segments of that new population persevered and excelled. Asian students quickly outperformed the masses and became some of our finest students. The backbone of success starts with the parents, and Asian parents were among the most demanding in our land. They continue to be. Other segments of our population lacked the drive to have their children do well and escape impoverished worlds of real problems. But most kids in school were allowed to become soft and lazy in the classroom as parents' focus went toward making life very comfortable for themselves and their children. They became complacent with the status quo in education and were hoodwinked by the jargon coming from the bureaucrats. It would be a long time before people in this country became seriously interested in having our students capable of competing on international levels.

It is important to take an aside here. The slipping SAT scores became a political football used incorrectly to judge whether one school district was better than another. The test was never designed for that purpose, but business people looking for a quick point of comparison quickly began to use it that way. The educational bureaucrats rightfully cried foul, but they in turn developed their own tests for student measurement. Now the norm across the land is to have students pass state-mandated exams to pass academic courses. This criterion has become the sole factor in assessing whether or not schools and teachers have been successful in a given year. No consideration is made for the socioeconomic makeup of a particular class. No consideration is given to the academic abilities or limitations of students. No one pays attention to the fact that a majority of our students come to school each day hungry, and many are afraid to go home at night. Certainly, school systems and teachers have to be held accountable to the community for their performance and the growth of students, but who determines the standards? Are our business leaders and politicians, many of whom have harmed our communities with poor decisions, the people to set the norms? I don't know the answers, but I do know that judgments based on a single test score are invalid.

Yet we cannot ignore other issues that continued across the land. We still had soldiers in Vietnam and war protestors on the streets. Matters changed quickly as the troops came home in 1972, and the Kent State shooting pretty well ended college campus protests. But rapidly there was a major leadership crisis in the land. In 1968 President Johnson recognized that the war in Vietnam would cost him reelection, and he declined to run. The campaign was bloody in the worst sense, and Richard Nixon became president. His vice president, Spiro T. Agnew, took on the press and publicly railed against anyone who was not conservative. It was only fitting to many that he came to an inglorious end when he was forced from office after pleading nolo contendere to charges of graft and corruption when he had been governor of Maryland. Then came Watergate, which, after a highly distasteful battle, cost Mr. Nixon his presidency. Clearly, there was a crisis of leadership in the land. Mr. Ford, the only president not elected directly to either the office of president or vice president, angered many in the land by pardoning Mr. Nixon. He justified his action by saying that the pardon was the only way to get the country to focus on something other than Mr. Nixon. He was probably right, but that action cost him reelection in 1976. Mr. Carter took office next, and he convinced no one that his efforts in office were worthy of another four years. He also had the misfortune of runaway inflation during his term.

And then there were drugs. They hit this country with a vengeance during this decade, and lives were altered forever. The workplace and the schools were hammered in ways they had never seen. Productivity suffered. Teachers faced problems in the classroom they had not seen before. Strange behavior, inattentiveness, disrespect in new forms, and many other weird patterns disrupted the normal flow of learning patterns. Our country lost too many good minds during that era to the evils of drugs, and we still do. We have to find ways to end the dependence on drugs in this country.

Back in the 1950s school district growth began through consolidation. That continued, but so did growth through explosive population growth. For example, in 1970, Charlotte, North Carolina, had approximately 240,000 people. Ten years later, it had 315,000, a 30 percent increase. All of a sudden there was a huge demand for school facilities and staff to add to the pressures caused by forced busing. These drastic and dramatic changes brought huge pressures to the schools.

Another change in the schools began to show itself. Many of the parents of young elementary students were themselves products of the lawless 1960s, and they had a dissolving desire to support the schools and show respect for the staffs. This problem would manifest itself more in the 1980s, but it was beginning to arise.

Across the country, standards continued to slip. For instance, the quality of automobiles produced in Detroit fell to new lows, and foreign cars began to appear on the roads in rapidly increasing numbers. Shifting populations, world market pressures, and plain human misbehavior took their toll on the old American way of doing things. Complacency resulting from a feeling that we were the most powerful and best in the world set in, and we became a soft nation. Times were changing and not for the better.

I was really excited to join the staff of a small well-established independent day school in Charlotte. My independent school background was the main reason I was hired because the school wished to strengthen that image in this market. What I did not know when arriving there was that there was mixed feelings among the parents about the type of instruction they wanted. A strong block wanted a very traditional independent school curriculum and instructional pattern. Another group looked toward more experimentation and newer patterns of teaching. A third wanted an extremely conservative reading program. The conservative block lost early as the other two outnumbered them when unified, as they did on this issue. In any case, there was room for experimentation in curriculum and teaching methodology. Later the school would meld several ideas into an absolutely first-rate independent school program.

There were good people and talented teachers in the English Department when I arrived, and we worked hard to strengthen the already solid academic program. We made students write regularly and developed their rhetorical, grammatical, and argumentative skills. We also read diverse works throughout the grades, strengthening students' critical reading skills. Curricular experimentation was in the air, and we tried new patterns. First, everyone in the department taught both junior and senior high grades. Not everyone in the department liked the idea, but the purpose was to have all of us involved in the continuum of English instruction from grades seven to twelve. The school was small enough at that time to teach this way, and we soon all learned the strengths and weaknesses of all students in all grades.

Another pattern we tried in the middle school curriculum was to develop learning blocks. For instance, each seventh grader would have to complete six learning segments. One might focus on grammatical and language building exercises. Another might emphasize learning to read short stories and poems critically. Another might focus on essay writing, etc. In any case, each student had to complete all six blocks. We developed all sorts of exercises on individualized projects. For example, in a vocabulary building exercise, students had to complete dictionary exercises, design and complete crossword puzzles, play Scrabble or other word games, and build personal dictionaries on new words that intrigued them. We had students review films as well as written works, etc. The details of these programs are long gone from my memory, but there's enough here to present the idea.

One year we did this in seventh grade, I discovered that some teachers wanted to teach some blocks but not others. Actually, it worked out that by pairing teachers at grade levels, we covered all the bases better than we would have otherwise because we used teachers to teach their strengths rather than their weaknesses. For example, I taught the blocks concerning language structure and development, and a less experienced taught the sections about literature. She felt more confident doing so, and her creativity in this area benefitted the students as did my experience in the study of language.

In the high school, our calendar was built on three terms rather than two semesters. As a result, we built a term-course curriculum. Each term, students could select the course they wanted to take. We did require that all tenth graders take an essay-writing course, and we suggested that some classes, such as Shakespearian tragedies, be taken at certain grade levels. We discovered that students took teachers rather than courses at each of the years.

I remember leading a workshop on curriculum design at some school conference and describing what we were doing. A participant raised his hand and said that if he introduced this idea at his school, he'd be shot as a communist. Another great comment came from a parent one night at a cocktail party. She came up to me and said that she'd sure like to talk to the idiot in the English Department who selected the books students read. I looked at her and replied, "You're talking to him." We became good friends even though our literary tastes remained incompatible.

Kids seemed excited by the program, and they continued to get into the colleges they and their parents wanted them to attend. I have no idea if any of the programs we designed remain in the curriculum, but I doubt it. The school's much larger with two campuses, and there have been several department heads in that department since I left years ago. But putting that program together was creative and fun.

Toward the end of my stay there, the school implemented a program named Mini-Mester. We took a week from the curriculum and implemented a series of weeklong activities students could choose from. There were several arts and craft activities, some cultural heritage programs, and all sorts of things I no longer remember. One of the most popular activities was called Charlotte at night, designed by Sue Van Landingham. She and a few other teachers took students to see all sorts of activities that happened at night. They visited a funeral home, participated on a radio talk show, visited the county jail, and did many other things as well. The kids particularly liked this program, and it was oversubscribed each year it was offered. In this day of end-of-the-year testing, there is not enough time in the school year for such a program. In this time of budget constraints, I suppose there would be no money as well.

Nobody ever knows exactly what turns a mediocre student into a good one, but we had a clear case of this Mini-Mester program doing that. There was a boy who excelled in cross-country but barely survived in the classroom. During Mini-Mester, he took a photography class and was totally turned on watching his negatives become prints. The process engaged him intellectually, and he took his awakening back to the regular classroom, where he became a strong student for the rest of his career. That success gave Mini-Mester credence, but it was short-lived as the school's academic direction headed back to a more conservative bent. It's too bad the program died because it also gave everyone a breath of fresh air in the middle of the winter.

I had never worked at a day school before and was pleasantly surprised by the close contact teachers had with parents. We regularly had parents on campus as volunteers, as fans at events and for conferences. In almost all cases, the contact strengthened bonds between the schools and the homes. We were an extended family, helping young people gain strength and wisdom. The parents were incredibly supportive of our efforts in most cases, but occasionally, there were the inevitable tensions.

One aspect of the school I particularly liked was that it had an honor system. On each paper, a student pledged that he or she had not cheated, etc. All cases of academic dishonesty and serious disciplinary issues went to a joint student-faculty discipline committee for review. The committee would hear the case and make a recommendation to the head of school for punishment if necessary. There were remarkably few hearings as the students lived by the code very well. Whenever there was a case, it was handled in a formal hearing done with great seriousness of purpose, and I can think of no case I heard where the recommendation from the committee was not followed by the head of school. The resulting actions intensified the sense of integrity on campus. Without that value, nothing else of worth can be taught. I, therefore, would insist on some sort of honor system involving student commitment in any school I were to run.

Only two negative cases stand out in my memory. In both, academic dishonesty was involved. It was clear to the committee that both students had cheated, but we could not prove either case successfully because both students lied at the hearing. Interestingly, both their fathers were noted attorneys in Charlotte, and I'm convinced that they had advised their sons to lie and taught them how to do so successfully. We had no choice but to dismiss the charges and exonerate the students, but I wonder to this day what values the fathers had taught their children. In both cases, the committee members had nothing to do with either student from that time forth.

Because the school was small and all the students knew one another when I arrived there, it was able to save money by not having lockers on campus. In each homeroom, there were cubbies without doors for students to store belongings, but they were seldom used. The kids carried their stuff around during the academic day and left it on piles in the courtyard between the academic buildings and the gym when they all were headed to meet their athletic commitment. It was uncanny to see girls' pocketbooks lying unguarded on the ground, but they were safe. Then the school began to grow rapidly, and suddenly there were many cases of theft. The trust disappeared as students did not know all the others well, and the drug culture made itself known on campus. As a result, lockers appeared on campus, and they signified a loss of innocence. We saw firsthand that bigger was not always better.

One other comment about the parents there: they were kind to faculty members they liked. On one occasion I was sitting in my office with a student, and there was a knock on the door. A mother stuck her head in, apologized for interrupting, and asked where my car was parked. I told her and thought nothing further of the incident until I climbed in the car at the end of the day and discovered a large cooked ham. Another set of parents welcomed me at their house and invited me to fish in their pond whenever I wanted. Such was the place.

Finally, the parents helped educate young faculty when we needed help. On one occasion I had assigned a term paper and given a due date. Students kept asking me about the deadline, and I flippantly said that it could be in my hands no later than 6:00 AM Monday morning. I awoke to the sound of running feet at the front door. Two weeks later, a father quietly told me never to do that again. In a second case, when I was the school disciplinarian, I suspended a student for a couple of days for some indiscretion. But I made a bad mistake by calling the father and suspending the boy over the telephone. His response was, "Okay, but, Pete, don't do such an important act over the phone. Do it in person." He was absolutely right. I had a lesson in humility, and we became good friends. The boy went on to be a fine rabbi.

Although the school had built a solid reputation over a period of time, political pressures caused it to make some changes to further improve its legitimacy and reputation. First, it decided to gain accreditation from the Southern Association of Schools and Colleges. Second, it decided that the faculty members should become certified by the State of North Carolina. Both steps were good in the Charlotte market because they gave the school even stronger standing in the academic community. At a time when new schools with unknown faculty were springing up almost daily, these moves made sense in solidifying the school's position in its market. Both steps brought me to new learning experiences.

I was selected to be head of the steering committee in the accreditation process. The task is not easy as members of the staff have to study each aspect of the school and make recommendations for improvement. The process takes time, and reports are voluminous. In the year we did our self-study, I learned our school inside and out, and I saw issues we had to resolve to become a truly fine academic institution. We were very close to that status, but we became stronger and better by undergoing the evaluation process. We also became more unified in our sense of direction and in our dedication to achieve excellence.

Because all my teaching experience had come at independent schools, there had been no need for me to gain state certification as a teacher, but the time had come. I enrolled in a local state university for the purpose. I think it took about two years of night courses to complete the requirement. In those courses I encountered many professors. Not one required much academic demand, and I did virtually no work to obtain the certification. I just put in time. In one course we spent most of our time off campus developing a project. It so happened that I was doing one for my school, and all I did for the university was to put in a file a copy of any paper I did for the school project. I never sorted the papers and made a twenty-minute report on the project. I even stopped going to class. For that I received an A. In other courses I knew the professors did not read the required papers, and I just made stuff up. While the papers were creative, they were not academic. This lack of academic seriousness and demand angered me after working like a slave to gain my MA in English at Lehigh University. Upon completing the requirements, I met with the then head of the department, a man I liked. I told him that the teachers in his department were perpetuating a fraud since they gave grades based on little or no required work. I also asked how any teachers they had trained could demand academic excellence when they had not experienced it themselves in a classroom. Needless to say, the talk did not go well. I must say that twenty years later I returned to the same university for graduate work in educational administration and encountered several professors who were serious about their work and demanding of their students. Maybe we had all grown up some. One positive note from this experience is that I met a neighbor who has been a very close friend of the family for more than thirty years. I also worked for her briefly when she was superintendent of our local school system.

Teaching usually brings about major learning experiences for the instructor. I had not taught girls before coming to this school, and a group of seventh-grade females exposed me to a behavior pattern that still causes me wonder. About six or seven girls created a taunting circle, but they tore apart one another rather than outsiders. One day Emily would be the target, and all the others would bully her unmercifully. The next day Nancy would be the victim, and Emily, who had just suffered, might well be the worst attacker. Not one girl was spared of this frightful behavior. They all cried and sought out Mrs. Abo, their motherly math teacher, who took them under her wing. Without Virginia Abernathy and Dolly Hickman, those girls would not have survived the seventh grade. Laura, the scrawniest of the bunch, suffered the most. The rest even stole her glasses from time to time. None of us could figure out what caused the bullying or how to stop it. Not even their mothers could break the pattern. Fortunately for the girls, seventh grade came to an end, and the group pattern did not reappear in grade eight.

About fifteen years later, the class had a reunion to which my wife and I were invited. As we walked through the parking lot, a lovely young lady met us. She said hello but did not identify herself.

I recognized her as Laura, and she asked me not to tell anyone else who she was. She also said that she really did not want to see the group but came to show her classmates what she had become. As the party progressed, she wandered through the crowd for quite a while without being recognized. Little by little, her classmates realized who she was and really welcomed her. As they did, her reservations about being there melted, and she truly had a good reunion. Although the results of the group meanness had taken a great toll on Laura, time and her own success allowed her to get beyond it. I'm glad I was there to see this healing.

Of all the faculty members at this school during my time there, the most focused and dedicated was John Cook, football coach. Not an articulate man, John had the uncanny ability to convince boys that they were unbeatable. Usually, his squad numbered about thirty, and many of the kids were small. But John taught them to be fierce and dedicated. One year he had a defensive end who weighed no more than 125 pounds. John convinced him that no one could beat him, and Stowe performed admirably. Because the school was K-12 and there was a strong PE program, the football staff was able to build player skills and personal relationships for many years. Thus, all boys knew the football system early on and could make moves instinctively. John also picked his competition well, playing both independent and public schools that would be competitive with his program. As he kept winning, he developed a strong following among students and parents, but he had two battles to face.

As the school grew, more boys wanted to play soccer rather than football. John, who was the athletic director as well as the football coach, wanted no part of a program that might cost him players. As the pressure built, he tried to have soccer as a spring sport, but he ran into problems with that idea because all other schools played it in the fall. Inevitably, he bowed to the pressure, and soccer became a full-fledged fall sport. Publicly he supported the program, but privately he continued to dislike it, especially when he lost a good athlete to soccer.

In his other battle he took on the mothers and lost. After soccer appeared on the sports schedule, there was pressure to have cheerleaders appear at those games as well as the football games. This issue became a problem as the cheerleaders would have to appear several nights a week, causing them academic difficulties. The pressure grew, and John tossed out a trial balloon: develop a subset of cheerleaders, secondary in status, to cheer at the soccer games. Suddenly there was a furor among the mamas. No secondary squad ever appeared, and the varsity cheerleaders worked out a way of cheering for both squads. John went very silent on the subject and beat a hasty retreat.

The school was saddened later when he met an untimely death riding his bicycle. His contributions to the school were wonderful, and the school fittingly honored him by naming the football field for him.

There were other strong teachers who led students to success. Ambie Vulgan was a really good math teacher we should never have lost, but he and the head of school butted heads. In that scenario, the teacher rarely wins. Ambie went on to greener pastures, and the Math Department missed him greatly.

Mary Todd and Frank Justice were the backbones of the English Department, and they taught with passion and success for many years, and the kids loved them and produced for them. Mary's passion for Shakespeare has been unwavering, and God knows how many kids she inspired to read his stuff. Frank counseled and laughed with hundreds of kids, making the school a better place.

And there were characters. Dave Wheeler taught PE to little kids and coached football. Virtually every boy from third grade on had been tagged with an absurd nickname by Dave, and they loved him. Our PE classes consisted of teaching lots of football skills, thus strengthening John Cook's program. One winter day Dave pulled out boxing gloves, and the kids had a great time whaling one another with huge gloves. About three days into that program, mothers started calling the head of the Lower School, and progression to building future Mohammed Ali's stopped. Too bad. Neither Jimmy Broadway nor I, who also taught third-grade PE, could live up to the status of Coach Wheeler, and we happily basked in his glow.

Mrs. Raoul, Mrs. Cobb, and Mrs. Beatty taught foreign languages with skill and charm, and their efforts were well appreciated by their students. Advanced students always placed well in AP exams and went on to study languages in college. They added class and grace to the faculty.

In the lower and middle schools were many wily veterans who sent well-qualified students to us in the upper school. There was at least one mother-daughter combination in the lower school, and a girl of the third generation was a student. Schools don't get much more family than that. I suppose now there are third—and fourth-generation students in the school, which speaks volumes about what it means to its clientele. In any case, the teachers of the youngsters were talented teachers and fun people. I enjoyed working and partying with them.

The strength of this faculty was its enthusiasm and commitment to the growth and well-being of its students. As a result, opinions and individuality were strong. We were encouraged to try new ideas and teach our way as long as student academic growth was clearly the outcome of our efforts. As a result, we tried ideas and talked about them both on and off campus. There was a healthy academic tension in the air, and we all grew. Teachers ranged from being loving grandmotherly to youngsters fresh out of school, learning along the way. We talked all the time about what worked and what didn't, and as a result, we felt energized by our efforts. Working there was fun for most of us, and many stayed there for thirty or forty years.

The school had a foundation used to bring in outside speakers. One year we invited Howard Nemerov, a former poet laureate of the United States. He was then a professor at Washington University in St. Louis, and he had the appearance and manner of an academic. In his presentation to the students, he showed a picture of a weathered barn door and began describing it. The more he talked, the more we began to see what he saw, and we realized that his vision was very different from ours. Instead of seeing just a weathered set of boards nearly falling off its hinges, Mr. Nemerov saw family struggle, years of effort, warmth, entry to family holdings, etc. As I listened, I began to see his vision. Suddenly I realized that we all see things differently and that we should pay more attention to the visions of others because we can learn from them. This lesson has helped me over the years in that it has helped me become more tolerant and open to new ideas.

I would still be at that school had there not been a turnover of heads of school. I loved working for the man who hired me, although he certainly was not without faults, but I quickly grew to have no respect for his successor and resigned. In retrospect, I made a bad mistake because I really liked the school and most of my associates. I was caught up in my own ambition and a lack of respect for a man who would not stay there long. I should have had the wisdom to understand that.

One final word on my experience there: the members of the board of trustees of that school were then and continue to be fine, dedicated people interested only in developing and maintaining a really good school. Their wisdom and stewardship have done so, and so have the school heads they have selected since I left. Over the years, they have led the school through a merger and growth, but the tradition of excellence remains strong and true.

During this decade, our children began their academic journeys. As a result, my wife and I found ourselves in the position of judging teachers from a parental perspective. One wonders how objective any parent is in this process because, after all, there is nothing more important to most parents than their children's well-being and success. Because each child is different, so must each journey be.

Our son began his educational journey at the school where I was working. His kindergarten year was wonderful because his teacher, an experienced pro and great teacher, knew exactly how to deal with him. His first-grade teacher, another seasoned pro, counseled us that he had a learning disability, which could be helped in the school's tutoring program. We agreed to enroll him in that, and every school day, he and a few others would leave their classroom to go to tutoring. Little did we know that our decision backfired because our son felt he had to get this special help for being stupid, which he is certainly not. As a result, he built a wall against classroom education that would last through his academic career. Interestingly, we did not discover the reason for his discomfort until years later when he was fighting in Kuwait with the US Marine Corps. One day when he was answering a letter from his grandmother, he suddenly felt a funny taste in his mouth. He realized that he always got that sensation when he wrote a certain word, and he wondered why. He put the letter aside, and wrote the word repeatedly until he realized that the taste was of a piece of candy he got at the tutoring center when he spelled that word correctly. Clearly, there was carryover from the tutoring session, but the negative effects outweighed the positive ones.

His lack of academic success led to many classic behavioral problems in school, and even today, twenty years later, there are middle school teachers who still shudder when his name is mentioned. He has gone on to a successful career, and he is the homework enforcer in his house. Furthermore, he is an avid reader, thus learning about all sorts of subjects. Somehow, despite his own negative experiences in schools, the importance of education got through his head.

His sister had the fortune of having a great teacher, whom she loved, for both first and second grades. As a result, she was off to a flying start on her educational trip. She has read everything in sight ever since, but as frequently happens, her academic path filled with missteps as ennui set in about grade four. I suspect that she can name few of her teachers, and those would probably not react kindly to her evaluation of their efforts and results in her behalf. She is a classic case of a bright student who rarely got challenged and, thus, rarely felt the need to perform well in the classroom. Like her brother, she has been a late bloomer who has gained real success in her work and community efforts. She also is the homework enforcer in her house, and her daughter has no chance to be a slacker.

Are my children and their teachers solely to blame for their academic issues? Of course not. I as a father did not pay enough attention to their academic problems. I use the excuse that I spent all day working with other kids and was tired at night. That excuse does not fly. The most important task I had during my life was raising my children properly, and in this area I did not live up to my responsibility. It is a cross I have to bear.

But as a teacher and a parent, I realize that understanding and motivating youngsters is not always an easy task, especially after they have had their egos adversely marked in schools. Being frustrated as a parent has no doubt made me a better educator because I understand a balance parents try to achieve with their children. We want to push our kids academically, but at the same time, we cannot let that area of life dominate and ruin all others. We need to be sure that the family bonds do not get severed in a conflict of issues between parent and child. I guess that means that I as a teacher became more empathetic with family problems.

Both our children went to schools for a majority of their education where academic challenge and good performance were not regularly demanded. Yes, there were children who went through the same schools and did very well, but there were many others who simply went through the motions without gaining any intellectual passion. More importantly, there are many who face the same problem today largely because the system fails them. Many schools fail because they do not adapt to the changing conditions in this world. But more about that later.

The 1980s: Deus ex Machina in Selfish City

The 1980s sort of rolled in without much ado. Yes, the extremely high interest rates of the late '70s fell some, but not enough to help major farmers in the early '80s when poor crop yields put them in conflict with the banks. Thousands lost their farms to the banks and conglomerates, which gobbled them up and created huge agricultural corporations, thus altering the mid-West forever, another move in the "bigger is better" mentality. President Reagan reasserted leadership by firing the striking aircraft controllers, but he also put this country in further economic stress by wild defense spending and the cutting of taxes for the rich. The decade drifted along without major drama or events other than the fall of the Berlin Wall. Even the stock market took a hit in the late '80s, concerning people about the economic well-being of the country. Our dependence on imports increased dramatically. Honda, Toyota, VW, etc., really worried Detroit automotive types, who were not paying attention to the desires of the marketplace. The demand for oil worsened, and the oil companies gobbled one another up. Big-name corporations of the past in this country continued to disappear because the products they made either became obsolete through technological improvement or because they were produced just as well or better by foreign corporations. WalMart, with its cheap, foreign goods, drove small retailers out of business and adversely altered Main Street forever. The banks continued to gobble one another up, and some people began to wonder what had happened to the Sherman Antitrust laws. A malaise of mediocrity seemed to cover the country, and it carried over to the schools, where academic standards kept slipping. Not much progress—other than medical and other scientific advances, notably in the computer world—was taking place.

Yet there was serious research being done in the academia on learning methods, learning disabilities, etc., which brought about far better understanding of the ways people learn. Little of that output caused change in curriculum and teaching methodology at this point, but it caused recognition that business as usual in the schools was going to have to change.

Some members of our society decided to do nothing but party, hang out, and escape. They felt no need to be responsible for their actions or their offspring. Dependence on government economic programs grew, and so did resulting resentment from the majority toward those who seem to show no responsibility for their own actions. Sale of intoxicants and illegal substances kept growing, and so did the need to "escape reality." More artists and musicians died through overdoses, and college and high school kids began binge drinking. This was really not an age to be remembered fondly.

A major societal issue began to appear in the schools as well. Many of the parents of elementary students had not felt challenged or successful in their educational programs. As a result, they had decreasing interest and respect for the schools and teachers. Community support began to erode, and parents began to blame the schools for their children's academic failings. The increasingly litigious society forced the courts into the schools, forcing further erosion of administrative authority. Teachers felt a lessening of support as school administrators feared making decisions that countered student or parent desire. Teachers felt left in a vacuum of support when handling unpleasant situations. As a result, they shied from handling them, giving students and parents more authority in schools. As parents demanded, they received with short-term gains resulting in long-term losses. Under parental pressure, many schools saw rampant grade inflation despite lessening academic achievement, causing employers and college instructors to conclude that students learned too little in high schools. Blame passing instead of acceptance became a mantra that has lived on.

I took a hiatus from teaching for about ten years, trying to find my fame and fortune in other arenas. People who knew me well said that I showed true animation only when I was talking about education or teaching. It was clear to them that I was out of my element away from schools. During this time, I was involved deeply in a nonprofit organization. I asked the head of another independent school to serve on the board of this activity with me, and in time he offered me a job at his school. I was a bit leery of going back to teaching after being out of the classroom for so long. As a result, I asked a former colleague about doing so, and he was skeptical of my success in returning because the educational world had changed a great deal in that time. After serious self-examination, I went back, and I'm glad I did.

This school, founded in 1970, was very similar to the one I had left, but the clientele, many of whom lived in the same neighborhoods as those of the other school, was different. My job there was to do college counseling and teach English. Both aspects of the job were interesting and challenging, and the dual demands kept me engaged and excited for another eight years.

While the focus of this work is on teaching itself, we have in other sections looked at factors affecting the art. As is the case of every school, the clientele, its desires, socioeconomic standing, and expectations have a huge impact on its culture. The students came from upwardly mobile families with lots of clout. The parents were used to getting things their way, and they expected the school to ensure that their students would go to the finest colleges and universities across the land. Most parents were realistic in evaluating their children's odds of getting into various colleges, and they worked well with the school to make those good choices become valid opportunities. Then there were others. I shall never forget my first day of employment there. A father introduced himself to me and said he had a son who was a senior. This boy was a fine student and a really neat kid whom I later discovered to be a viable candidate for all highly competitive schools. The father told me that his son had applied to Princeton, and if he did not get in, the father would have my job. That introduction set the tone for much of my college counseling stint there. Interestingly, the boy was accepted by Princeton but chose not to attend. Rather, he accepted a Morehead Scholarship at the University of North Carolina at Chapel Hill. I never heard a word from his father after that, and I'd just as soon never encounter him again.

A mother of a candidate to Wake Forest once told me that she had almost finished her son's application there. Now how much integrity was involved in that candidacy for admission? Yet another parent called me one Christmas morning to be sure that all the arrangements for his upcoming college tour were in place. When I tried to call him back, of course, he was not available. It was clear to me that many of the parents at this school thought the staff there to be their personal servants. I resented that assumption.

Seeing this attitude was interesting in that I had known this school from its beginning. In the early days, the parents did whatever they could to help make it a fine place. It was not uncommon to see parents on Saturday mornings planting trees or flowers or doing whatever else needed to be done. As the school matured, the attitude of the parents changed to that of being served rather than that of serving. This phenomenon is not uncommon in new institutions. As the original, founding group ages out, the successive ones have not experienced the need to help the school. Instead, they become consumers: "They pays their money and takes their goods." As a result, there is a totally different attitude from the parents toward the school—one found common almost anyplace—and it is not flattering. The faculty felt it, and with reason. History at this school shows that the unhappiness by a parent or two could cost a faculty member his job, fairly or unfairly. As a result, many teachers were made to feel that they existed purely in a servile world, and as a result, they were not willing to try new techniques that might well improve their students' educational experience. Yet the school grew and improved under the tutelage of its long-term fifth headmaster. Undeniably, he built a fine school, albeit with some flaws.

Yet in this milieu there came a bright light: the personal computer—deus ex machina, the machine from the gods. This school, as did many others, spent money to bring the computer to the classroom, and it made all the difference to me as a teacher. With the help of Sylvia Knapp, whom I can never thank enough, I had an epiphany. Here was a tool that took away the physical agony of writing and allowed easy rewriting. Here was a tool that allowed students to create papers that built their pride rather than fear. Here was a tool that allowed students to experiment easily with sentence construction or placement as they wrote. Furthermore, here was a tool that produced papers easy for me to read and evaluate. Good-bye eyestrain from reading poor penmanship. There was yet another dynamic about the computer I didn't realize until later.

My first success story with the computer came early on. I had assigned a paper to a class of seniors to write about something that created passion within them. Tim turned in a virtually illegible paper with the opening line of, "I hate Dr. Campbell"(who was the head of the English Department). I told Tim that although Dr. Campbell, who had taught Tim junior English, was a friend of mine, Tim had every right to hate him but that he ought to write a paper that truly showed the hatred. I said that I could not make heads or tails out of the ideas expressed because they were totally illegible. I then told him never again to submit a paper not produced on the computer. Soon a rewrite appeared that was legible and reasonably coherent. We discussed the new version, and Tim went back to work. After another session on the computer, Tim clearly showed why he hated Dr. Campbell and, thus, fulfilled the assignment successfully. Soon Tim and many of his classmates began producing drafts of assignments before the due date. It was not uncommon for me to hear a student hollering my name down the hall between classes because they had a draft they wanted to show me. We'd discuss it, and the students would go back to work. As a result, the quality of the submitted papers improved dramatically, and the value of rewriting was impressed upon the students. Reading the drafts made my job of evaluating the final papers much easier because most of the errors had been dealt with earlier. Tim went on to write consistently decent essays his senior year. So did the rest of his peers.

Early in any course, I'll have students write a paper, generally about something in their realm of experience. I'll grade and return it only to have them rewrite it. Thus, they see early on the value of rewriting. One year in a class, the second edition of the papers did not reach an acceptable level of craftsmanship, and I had the students do another rewrite. One boy was really angry about my assignment, and he voiced his opinion loud and clear. I held fast, and as we worked on the papers in the computer lab, I heard Matt suddenly say, "I understand what he means and wants." For him this class was a major breakthrough because he went from being a lazy, competent student to a self-demanding star, who later attended Dartmouth College. The computer, which makes editing quite easy, clearly enables students to fix errors in syntax and thought to create really significant papers.

The third example of the computer's use as a tool came from a very different path. I learned that one of my students had significant learning disabilities that greatly hindered his study of languages. Yet he was very bright, and he loved computers. His writing skills improved dramatically when he figured out how to use the computer to his advantage, and he became an A student in my class. He also used the tool to study a foreign language and did well. He matriculated at North Carolina State University and was graduated with honors in his major of electrical engineering. Without the computer, he could never have been accepted by that university.

I learned of another advantage to having students write their papers in the computer lab while I was there. I could move around the room and give each student pointers during the class time. That one-on-one attention did more to improve their writing skills than did group lectures about writing techniques or theory. Also, I knew who actually wrote the papers. Sometimes the authorship was questionable when the papers were written at home.

I became a total convert to the use of the computer or word processor as a tool for teaching and producing writing. Time has proven my pioneering to be wise as more and more student writing is produced on computers. In fact, the machine is so widely used by some school districts that students rarely use paper and pencil. The college where I currently teach is trying to become a paperless campus, thus forcing students to submit papers via the Internet and instructors correcting them electronically and returning them the same way. The institution is saving vast amounts of money spent on paper with students gaining the same or better service. Furthermore, we're helping to save vast numbers of trees.

With the Internet at their fingertips, students can now write serious and valid research papers without ever entering a library. The Web gives them access to materials they can gain without picking up books or scholarly journals. Sitting here, I have at my beck and call more scholarly material about the subject of my master's thesis than

I did at the three university libraries I used. Yes, there is a danger that students can submit papers fraudulently produced, but most instructors worth their salt can find those pretty easily. The plus side here is that students have access to vast amounts of information to support claims and relationships they are making. Hence, they can write better and far more interesting papers.

While I worked at this school, Mother Nature brought her ferocious presence to bear in the Carolinas in October of 1989. Hurricane Hugo hit land. Moving very fast after landing on the South Carolina coast, it hit Charlotte, North Carolina, early the next morning. The devastation it caused was unbelievable as stately oak trees and their peers were torn every which way from the ground. As a result, parts of the communities were devastated, power was lost for several weeks, and schools were closed for several days as people in the community did whatever they could to clear roads and restore normal life. Teachers reported strange student behaviors once schools reopened. Those of us teaching high school felt as though we were restarting the year. The unnatural break had broken normal student concentration, forcing us to review before proceeding with new course work. Elementary teachers commented that many students were so terrorized by the storm that they had to be made to feel safe before they could begin learning again. Bad dreams in small heads ran rampant for a while in the area. I suspect we faced a mild version of what teachers face daily in war-torn parts of the world. We were inadequately prepared to cope with these problems, but we did the best we could.

Hurricane Hugo created incredible damage to North Carolina, and it caused most of us to operate well out of the norm as we recovered. Some, of course, bore the brunt of the damage, and in this particular and odd case, the wealthy got hammered because the giant trees in southeast Charlotte fell, causing unbelievable messes. Despite the damage, people reacted positively by helping one another out and working together. Yet there were scenes from the theater of the absurd. For example, about thirty-six hours after the hurricane had hit, I drove across Charlotte to get the pile of papers I needed to grade. I drove through what seemed like a war zone to reach the school where I worked only to find a football game going on. I could not believe that in a city with all its devastation the school powers felt maintaining a football schedule was more important than helping one another solve some pretty huge problems brought about unexpectedly by a massive storm. Almost twenty-five years later, I still don't.

Before leaving a discussion of this decade, I must comment on my children's academic experiences. Both continued their trek through the local public school system with disappointing results. I have to take some of the blame as a parent for not pushing them as hard as I should, but the basic problem with their schooling was that they were bored stiff in school. Our son got away with using the same two books for required book reports during several years, and our daughter just read what she wanted. There was little to no demand of them in the classroom, and there seemed to be little discipline in the high school. Both kids did minimal work, and our son skipped regularly without our knowledge. Both went on to college, but neither finished. Happily, they did pick up a strong work ethic and have been very successful in the workplace. Interestingly, both are the homework enforcers in their houses. So maybe their academic experiences weren't as bad as I thought.

I have not spent much time over the years looking at the progress of that local school system, but several of my neighbors have worked for it, and judging by them and the rising test scores of the system, progress has been made. I hope so for the sake of the families with students matriculating there. I do know that the neighboring school system has improved dramatically over the past ten years. Two of our grandchildren go there, and they have done very well and seemed to be challenged regularly.

My children's academic experiences leave me empty and angry as a parent because I feel that nobody in the system really cared about either child. Both seemed to attend institutions that had little control over their learning experiences and even behavior. I'm sure that teachers at those places took a dim view at our role as parents as well. There was an almost total lack of communication between institutions and parents about the academic experience of my children. I have vowed as a teacher that no such gap should ever appear in my relationships with students.

So in this decade of mediocrity, there was a huge, bright star—the use of the computer in the classroom. It would lead us to the next decade of instruction with hope for improved instruction and learning. But the negatives would not go away; nor would others in the world.

The 1990s: A World of the Haves and the Have-Nots

The '90s was a decade of tremendous economic prosperity for most, and people reacted by spending madly, thus building the GNP. But there was a problem with that spending in that people used credit rather than cash. They built huge debt, which did not seem to worry them in this period of prosperity. The prevalent attitude was, "I want it now and will pay for it later." As long as the economy was growing, this strategy seemed okay, but there were warning clouds on the horizon. For example, many college students took out student loans and were faced with massive payments for a long future. As the prices of cars grew rapidly, financing plans allowed for five—and six-year loans to keep the payments within reach of the buyers. The downside was that the finance charges added huge costs to the car, and frequently the vehicle was well worn out before it was paid for. The real estate world played the same game by offering balloon mortgages, which had dire consequences five years later if the buyer's income level had not improved dramatically. Finally, the American lifestyle caused most families to need two wage earners, and thus, there were fewer moms at home to greet their children returning from school.

Furthermore, the days of American economic self-dependence was over. We had become deeply involved in the global economy, creating dramatic changes in our economy. To compete internationally, companies had to change the ways they did business and do heretofore unthinkable things to heighten profits. WalMart, followed quickly by other international big-box stores, changed the retail world, effectively killing off small stores. We imported more and more goods, thereby eliminating the need for many of the small manufacturing plants, which had provided jobs all over the country. NAFTA and other trading alliances helped kill off the small plants as well. International corporations sent jobs to foreign countries to lessen labor costs. They also improved their technology by installing computer-driven machinery and robots to improve productivity and become more globally competitive. General Electric Corporation, under the leadership of Jack Welch, showed the business world the need to change its business model totally to survive and grow in this new global economy. Firms with less talented leadership found it harder and harder to compete. Companies swallowed up other companies in order to get big enough to compete, and we were about to see that bigger is not always better. The automotive industry, which began having troubles with foreign imports in the '70s, should have been examples of problematic issues with blind growth, but we didn't watch. Nor had we watched when the domestic steel industry began to decay and die because of imports and excessive overhead. In general we as concerned citizens didn't pay enough attention to the economic bad decisions that would come to haunt us.

This country has been built by immigrants. Virtually every family here, except those of the Native Americans, is the product of immigrants. From the beginning of this country, most people came here for freedoms and opportunities not found elsewhere. One notable exception was the block of African Americans who were imported for the economic well-being of others. People from all over the world have arrived here, planted themselves, worked hard, prospered, and have been accepted. In the '90s immigration exploded as demand for cheap labor skyrocketed across the land. Unfortunately, far too many people came illegally, creating all sorts of social issues today. As we look toward the future, we have to see that immigration is going to continue, and it will help this country grow, but it has to be controlled properly to eliminate the crush of illegals crowding areas of our country.

But immigration brings huge social pressures to society, especially in the world of education. Elementary teachers face daily the problem of communicating with children whose primary language is not English and whose social customs may be vastly different from those of more traditional students. School districts in major urban areas have student bodies in which white students are in the minority and which have more than 50 percent of students below the poverty line. Teaching in schools with student mixes like these is a very complex and difficult task.

Another issue facing secondary schools in the '90s was that admission to colleges became more difficult for many students. The finest colleges and universities drew far larger application pools from which they accepted the same number. For example, Harvard University now accepts about 8 percent of its applicants. Thirty years ago they accepted about 20 percent. Seventy years earlier it took almost all its applicants. Major state universities had the same kind of shrinking acceptance rates. Those, along with the rapidly increasing private college costs and the expanding pool of viable applicants, caused the second tier of state university systems to explode in growth. Yet they too now have fierce competition for admission.

In this decade, the sense of entitlement grew. Too many people, students included, wanted to achieve goals without effort. They expected to gain whatever they wanted simply because it was their right. A college friend spent his whole career teaching biology in a public school system outside Pittsburgh, Pennsylvania. One year one of his female AP biology students told him that poor grades in this class were harming her self-image. She was not amused when he suggested that the best way for her to improve that self-image was to study. Grade inflation became a fact of life at many competitive schools. The independent school where I worked had an average grade of B because Cs caused so much flack teachers did not want to give them even when deserved by the students. Parents expected that children should receive B's just because the tuition had been paid. What happened to the concept espoused in an E. F. Hutton commercial, "We make money the old-fashioned way: we earn it"?

The school I worked for, as do most, catered to the happiness of its clients. I guess doing so made economic sense as happy students do not transfer to other schools, thus ensuring the health of the bottom line. Each year, the senior class took a trip over spring break. Such a concept has a long and honorable tradition in the history of schools. For example, many kids in this country got to see the wonders of Washington, DC, or New York that way. Well, at this school, the trips grew in grandeur as the years passed. As we examine this issue, we must remember that the school had in place an honor-and-discipline policy that, among other things, forbid students to partake of drugs or alcohol either on or off school grounds. Needless to say, the policy was broken regularly, but students were rarely punished for their transgressions in this area. Someone had the bright idea to have the class go on a cruise for their trip. Somber voices tried to suggest that putting students on a ship solely designed for hedonistic pleasures was not a good idea. The temptations available to them would put them in direct conflict with a school policy that, if broken, could result in the expulsion of the students involved. The naysayers were ridiculed and beaten down by the wisdom of the times that the students were products of Charlotte's finest, that they knew how to behave, and that the school chaperones would guarantee good behavior.

Well, guess what! The stories that returned from the cruise clearly told that many students had indeed succumbed to hedonistic temptations and had fallen off the rightful path. There were also clear tales that the most senior chaperone himself had imbibed with students. What a mess ensued. A couple of kids became scapegoats and did get tossed from school. Some others received a lesser punishment, but the bulk went scot-free. Furthermore, the lead chaperone received no punishment at all. In fact, shortly he was promoted to a headmastership of another school. The head of school, to the knowledge of the faculty, never received a reprimand for allowing such stupidity to take place. One highly respected faculty member whose daughter went on the cruise resigned in outrage. Others of us felt that the whole scene was a prime example of noblesse oblige. If we do not value the safety and well-being and try to develop strong moral behavior in our students, what good is the school?

Yet nationally a positive trait continued without much fuss in the public. Curricular experimentation continued, new means of classroom delivery were explored, and the critics of the educational bureaucracy continued to cry out about problems within the schools that were not being addressed. Business leaders spoke for greater needs of improving academic performance necessary to develop and maintain employees skilled enough to keep our firms competitive. Yet community leaders were loath to change because they feared the unrest and costs caused by change. Too few saw the parallels between the results of maintaining a status quo in education to the same done in industry during the late '60s and '70s, when major national corporations fell to foreign competitors for failure to adjust to changing times.

For the early part of this decade, I remained where I was, teaching English, guiding students on to college, and doing whatever else I was asked. I also decided to go back to school, seeking a PhD. I returned to the local state university, which was in the process of gaining its own PhD program and had, as a result, ended its association with UNC-Chapel Hill for that degree. I took all the courses available but never did get the PhD because the local school was delayed in gaining its program. The courses were interesting, and while I'm sorry not to get the degree, I'm glad I returned to school and saw the maturation of that program.

The English Department at the school employing me focused on teaching students to write strong, effective essays, and there was a core of faculty well capable of doing so. Many of us were also writing our own works, and we passed material back and forth, seeking wisdom and guidance from one another. We also had a woman on staff who was a superb editor, and she helped all of us. In a sense, our activity was like a writing camp, and the synergism that came from it brought about some very good, diverse experimentation and publication. We strengthened one another's confidence in our writing ability and opened us to a willingness to try new avenues. For example, I began experimenting with writing poetry, an interest that remains with me today.

Probably the most important aspect of our writing was that we carried our enthusiasm and improving craftsmanship into our classrooms. We asked more from our students in their essay writing, and as a result, their skills improved pretty dramatically. In effect, through our own writing, we became better teachers.

Having never taught in public schools, I was really interested when I received an invitation to become an assistant principal in a good public school system. The offer was heightened by the superintendent's desire to alter the program dramatically and have the district become a leading one in North Carolina. The focus was twofold: one, to have a flexible calendar for the school year, thus maximizing facilities and staff; two, to offer three-hour classes, which would result in a student's completing a course in a semester, thus intensifying instruction and allowing greater student choices of course offerings. I was intrigued by the offer as it was an opportunity for me to be involved in programs I had been reading about. I have always liked trying new ways and means of education for the benefit of the students.

Once again I took on a new life, but this time I did not realize how ill-prepared I was for the daily life in a world in which I had never taught. Nor did I realize that the school system was just beginning to make these changes, and there was a lot of resistance within the school and community at large. I spent my days taking attendance, monitoring discipline issues, ensuring that the buses cleared the place on time and that students left the school without creating mayhem on one another or their vehicles. I also discovered that many of the students came from worlds I had never experienced. Too many came to school hungry in the morning. Too many came from houses where no one cared for or about them. Too many came from homes where there were no expectations for success. Too many had little or no hope. Yet they came, and most worked as well as they could with teachers who cared about them and their progress.

I missed the interaction of the classroom, and I was not a good detail person trying to do a job that demanded one. But I loved the kids who were there. Most were funny and unpretentious, and most treated the school as a place where they did their thing, whatever that might be. The second year I was there, I did get to teach a ninth-grade English class, which had driven out two other teachers that year. Surprisingly, we had little problem, and the students scored very well on the end-of-year test. Everybody was pleased about that.

After several years, the system did adopt one of the programs it wanted. The plan was to offer both a regular and a year-round option for students The school calendar issue proved to be too complicated and costly to do in the high school, and after a few years, the dual calendar disappeared in the elementary and middle schools as well. The three-hour-class plan was put into effect and operates today. It works well and has been helpful in improving student testing results.

The district has gone well beyond that stage of experimentation in that now all students from third grade on receive a laptop computer. This program has brought the district national attention as a leader in curriculum experimentation. Two of my granddaughters are students in the district, and their parents are well pleased with the program and results.

I realized that I didn't fit the job I was doing and went back to the school where I had come from. I taught English rather than doing "administrivia" and liked the change. I would probably have finished my teaching career there had I not made a bad error of judgment. The school rightfully suggested that there were other places for me to play. I found a couple away from teaching and enjoyed them, but people who knew me well knew my heart was in teaching. Somehow, ten years later I found my way back in a very different venue.

It's funny how circles turn, and we stay intertwined with issues central to our life when we least expect it. One night just as I was starting my lawn service, I was mowing the lawn of my first customer. I looked across the vacant lot between the yard I was mowing and the next house. Across it walked a woman filled with determination, headed straight for me. She said that she was having a party two nights later and that her lawn service could not mow her yard until the night after the party. She asked me if I could, and I said yes. She gave me a long list of work to do; I got it done, and she hired me as her lawn service. Over the course of a year, I discovered that she was head of a local charter school, and she learned of my background in education. Not long afterward, I was asked to serve on the board of directors for the American Renaissance Charter School in Statesville,

North Carolina. I happily served on that board for several years, learning a great deal about the charter school movement. I helped two young people gain jobs on the faculty there, and both served with distinction. One left after about five years to assume a very responsible position in a local Christian school, and the other spent nine years at the charter school.

My experience there taught me that optional public schools, if properly run and having strong faculties, can be legitimate public school options for children who might not fare well in larger schools. The American Renaissance Charter School has served Statesville well and has gained a rightful place in the educational framework of that city. Performance of the students there continues to be good and to improve, and I'd like to think that those of us who were pioneers in this school set a good tone at the beginning of its operation, thus helping this school both grow and improve. Clearly, fate would not let me stray too far from service in the educational arena.

2000 Plus: The New Century

The year 2000 began with people holding their breaths waiting to see if all the computer systems would crash. Of course they did not, but many con artists came into the new century with big bucks bilked from those who had fallen to fear catered by the bilkers. What a way to start! 9/11 shook America. Then came Enron, the first of the big economic hits brought about by cheats. Bill Clinton balanced the budget, the last president to do so, but he had difficulty keeping his moral compass straight. The steroid scandal hit baseball, illegal immigration ran rampant, and church attendance continued to drop. Oh yes, there were also George W. Bush's imaginary "weapons of mass destruction" and his declaration that the war had been won. Greed ran rampant until the financial world nearly collapsed because of its own shady dealings. Along came the government to bail them out because "they were too big to fail." The big hitters in the financial industry took the government money, put it in their own pockets, and called good loans on small business owners, frequently putting them out of business. The government, despite screams from the Republicans, did bail out the auto industry, thus avoiding putting millions of workers on welfare. Unemployment grew rapidly, and workers who had lost their jobs through no fault of their own scrambled to survive. The hope engendered by the election of a dynamic, young black man withered because he, or anyone else for that matter, could not wave a magic wand and fix all the ills.

Today the masses struggle onward in continued economic difficulty while the 1 percent gets rapidly richer. The gap between the haves and the have-nots has become a gulf and is headed toward being a chasm. After working in the business world in the landscaping and trucking industries, I came back to teaching when I should be retired. Mitchell Community College in Statesville, North Carolina, offered me a position as an adjunct instructor, and I accepted. Am I glad I did because this experience has brought me back to the classroom I love, and it has given me students who are really appreciative of the efforts I put forth in their behalf. Teaching has also brought me back to writing; hence, here we are.

The community colleges in this land are a very important piece in the educational continuum in that they serve a group of students who would otherwise be lost. Most offer GED programs for those who dropped out of school. At the same time, many have accelerated programs for strong high school students who can earn an associate's degree in only one year beyond high school. The bulk of the students, however, are adults of all ages seeking an education to improve their state in life. It has not been uncommon for me to have classes with students ranging in age from fifteen to sixty plus, thus creating some interesting pedagogical challenges. Most community colleges have broad offerings from college transfer courses to professional training programs of all sorts. Many students are enrolled through the aegis of the Employment Security Commission, which pays their tuition for job retraining. Therefore, these institutions have larger student bodies than most people think, and the growth of those student bodies in the last decade has been phenomenal. As a teacher, I have been energized particularly by students who are returning to school after a gap of twenty years or more. Most come to night classes and are eager to learn. They do their assigned work and want to please. I have found that they respond remarkably well to praise and support from me. Once they gain their confidence in their ability to perform the tasks asked of them, they do better than their younger counterparts.

Many of these students have been badly battered by life, and they have horror stories to tell. But they are more than survivors; they want better from life, and they are willing to work. They are optimistic about their futures. Many major in fields such as nursing, police work, early childhood development, etc., areas whereby they can help their fellow man. These are tough, resilient, optimistic people, and I am honored to be able to help them along.

As I rapidly approach seventy, I am content being an adjunct instructor because I lack the energy and desire to be tied to a full workweek. Besides, I have many other interests that take my time. But I enjoy being in the classroom and watching the progress of student use and understanding of our language. I enjoy hearing their stories and feeling their energy as they march on. I'll keep spending time with students as long as I am able and welcomed by my current employer. Despite the political and economic mess we are currently suffering, I remain optimistic about our future because of the students who keep coming through my classroom doors.

Over the many pages so far, dear reader—to use a Victorian technique—you have followed a rather peripatetic career and maybe wondered what this narrative is all about. Well, it is background for several observations and conclusions that follow. Thanks for your patience.

Part II

Ponderings

Prologue to Ponderings

No journey is worth taking if it fails to generate thought and improvement. My educational trek has done both for me, and it has raised more questions than answers. What follows is a collection of random thoughts about the state of education in this country as I see it. There is no task in this country more important than that of education, simply because it will determine our success as a country and as individuals in the future. Therefore, we as a society have to take the improvement of this function to heart and improve it in ways we have not yet considered. Hopefully, this exercise of mine can help us as a nation move toward improving this important function. To end my journey without making some comments about it would render it ineffectual and unworthy, and so here goes.

Good Teachers

For the past several months, I have asked students, friends, peers, and other assorted souls what qualities are found in good teachers. The responses, while not scientifically collected or tabulated, point to remarkably few characteristics. Upon reflection, they seem obvious and natural. Clearly not all good teachers have all the qualities listed below, and those they do have are mixed according to the teacher's personality and interests. The traits are not listed in any order of importance either.

1. Good teachers are passionate people. They have strong interests in all sorts of subjects. They believe adamantly that others should share their passions. For example, even before my wife Gwen and I were married, my mother taught her to love birds. This introduction has given my wife a lifelong love and desire to study them. She says that only bird watching gives her a true relaxation. She spends hours studying bird books and computer programs about birds, and she has wandered in many places around the world seeking sightings of birds new to her. I expect my mother never realized the joy she gave my wife with this gift, but it clearly was a gift of passion. I cannot tell you how many people Gwen has turned on to birds. Paul Reardon, my swimming

coach in college and a thoroughly decent and nice man, led me to a sport in which I was active until my shoulders would no longer let me swim. Mary Todd, a former colleague in Charlotte, still carries her passion for Shakespeare and is asked to lead groups of older readers through the magic of the Bard's plays. Most of us have a memory of a teacher with a strong zest for life, and we realize we were better off for encountering that person.

2. Good teachers are people who are comfortable with who they are. They don't try to be anyone but themselves. They assess the teaching situation in which they find themselves, and adapt to it. They bring their strengths to whatever program the school pushes and make them work. Students know almost instantly teachers who are real and who are not. They are welcoming to the first, and they close doors to the second. It matters little to a student if the teacher is a dumpy, little soul or he-man as long as he or she is consistently the same person. Real people get real results.

3. Good teachers are demanding. They lay out goals and insist students meet them if they are to succeed. As students strive to meet those standards, they appreciate the mind—stretching resulting from their effort. They finally understand and value the goals themselves as being truly worthy of the effort put forth. They also know they are prepared to face the next set of challenges. In a sense, the course has been a worthy opponent that has been vanquished, and the victor is a better person for having fought the fight.

4. Good teachers are compassionate. They generally like students and want them to succeed. After all, each failure of a student is a failure of the teacher as well. In an unhappy scenario of course failure, there has not been effective communication between the two, and the effort of both has been wasted. I have encountered many teachers who seem to take pride in a certain number of failures in their course because they indicate that the course is tough. I've known teachers to fail students who have missed an arbitrary passing grade by as little as half a point. To me, a failure is a failure, and teachers are paid to present a syllabus in such a way that the student gains, not loses. I have known teachers who have been greeted warmly by students years after having had them in class. In fact, I've even known students who married former teachers. Such situations are rare, but student-teacher friendships are not. Sometimes good teachers try hard to remain personally aloof from students, but the compassion comes through during times of extra help or unexpected support. Good teachers are good people who like, respect, and urge their students. They also know that **each student is the most important person in the room**.

    One of my fraternity brothers told me of an experience he had with a history professor. George had not done well on his latest history test, and one day while walking across campus, he met his professor who told him that he was sorry he could give George no more credit on the test. George felt that the professor spoke in earnest, and he convinced himself to study history harder and become a better student. The professor had reached out in a way that made George feel important to the man. George responded positively. Maybe it is not accidental that because George felt so strongly about his experience in college, he later became a member of the board of trustees of that institution.

5. Good teachers are positive people. After all, it is their job to build student skills and knowledge. To do so, they have to be supportive of students, especially those who have difficulty. As long as the students put forth the required effort, good teachers bend over backward to push them along. I have heard bad teachers put down students or tell them they are not smart enough to be in this class. Those teachers should be fired on the spot.

6. Good teachers are adaptable people. They have to be. Each class is different. Texts change. Technology forces teachers to do their thing differently. Teachers have to move to different classrooms or even new buildings. A teacher may teach Algebra 1 to one class first period and to another just before lunch. Believe me, the attention span of students at those two times of the day are very different. Sometimes teachers have a plan of attack for a class and realize that it is just not working. So they have to go to plan B or plan C or plan . . .

7. Good teachers never stop learning. They are curious about all sorts of things. Sometimes students put them on to ideas that intrigue them. Most study their profession to become better at it. Some experiment or challenge themselves simply

because they cannot help doing so. Most want to know more about the world they live in just because it seems necessary to do so. They have passions that need to be fed so they can continue being passionate.

8. Good teachers are fair. They treat each student with the same degree of respect and hold all students to the same standards. Because we are all people, we encounter some students we like or dislike more than others. Life works that way. It should matter not whether teachers like or dislike any given student, but it matters that all students are treated fairly and respectfully every day.

9. Good teachers inspire. They create interest in students and cause them to want to learn more. They urge students to write better essays or clearer lab reports. More importantly, they cause them to question and create. They teach them to reach for a higher level of expectation and understanding. Finally, if they have done their job well, they demand their students to excite others and help them reach for new horizons. This quality is the ultimate of a good teacher. Those who possess it become truly great teachers.

10. They are collegial. They work well with their peers and the administration because they like working where they do and they want to improve their schools. While Lone Rangers serve their purposes occasionally, educational institutions are places where working together frequently brings synergistic results benefitting everyone involved. Furthermore, most teachers are gregarious souls who like working together.

These qualities are timeless. In developing my list, I have concluded that good teachers from any era could be put into a classroom in a totally different era and be just as successful. For instance, Plato could come to 2012 and turn on students while a great first-grade teacher here could go back to the 1400s and do well. Yes, there would be learning curves in all cases, but the strengths of the teachers would win out. The qualities of good teachers are timeless, and so are the results of those who possess them.

One final note on this topic: Good teachers give more than the results of any year-end test can show. Teaching is not a one dimensional activity. Students who are lucky to have good or great teachers gain multi-dimensional skills and advance in many different ways over the course of a school term. No two students in any class come to the year with equal skills, interest levels, creativity, maturity level, or confidence. Good teachers take all those differences into account while working with students, and they try their damndest to have each become a better student and learner. The task is multi-dimensional, and juding a teacher's skill simply by applying a score of a standardized test is not a fair measure.

What criteria should a teacher be evaluated by? The question is age-old, and many parties besides teachers have stake in the answer. Members of the schools and communities have to work together in developing these criteria, More importantly, the same people have to create the goals of educational achievement for their community. Leaving that job to some accrediting body, the state board of education, or even the federal government is an abdication of community responsibility. Until each community agrees on an educational plan and a set of standards by which that plan and its teachers are evaluated, everyone in the community will be disappointed in the results of the school. When teachers have helped in developing thoat plan and those criteria, they will feel that any resulting evaluation of their work will be fair. Oh yes, there is one more thing. Teachers expect to gain fair salaries and increases for their efforts. They also expect the groups paying them to stand behind their word and actually pay them what they have promised. To not do so is to break a vital trust of word, thereby breaking integrity.

What Great Teachers Do

If we have been lucky in our educational journey, we have encountered a great teacher—one who stands above the others. There are too few just as there are too few greats in any field, but they leave a lasting impression. Why else would the names of Socrates and Plato be well remembered after thousands of years? I'm not sure I ever encountered a teacher who was great for the whole term, but I have met some who have had great days or weeks. They have created lasting impressions and give me the temerity to try to comment on what they do and what they accomplish.

First, great teachers open minds. They cause explorations in new arenas; they excite curiosity. In a sense, they blow away student limitations by exposing them to a passion that demands attention. That fire may come from the love of mathematic or musical orderliness, the possibility of scientific discovery, the beauty of a line on a paper, the appreciation of great literature, or simply, the joy of life. In any case, that passion rules the teacher, and students feel it enough to willingly enter that instructor's world and partake of it. The resulting excitement leads the neophyte to his own world of magical discovery, causing him to reach new heights of effort and endeavor. I go back to my college days when I discovered that Dr. Branton did not read the Victorian poems we were studying; he lovingly recalled them from his memory. His ability to do so blew me away. How could a person love something that much to commit thousands of lines to his memory? In graduate school I studied Shakespeare one summer. We read a play a day, and the class was phenomenal. The professor, who was used to teaching this course as a lecture to 250 students, had eight in this session. He rocked back in his chair, put his feet on the table, and discussed matters of Shakespeare for hours on end. We were free to ask questions and rebut issues, and the professor taught us more than he ever knew. He challenged us to feel Shakespeare, to cry or laugh with him, to feel jealous anger or passionate love. Moreover, he quietly insisted that we gave vent to passionate feelings in class.

Second, great teachers make students become intellectually passionate and curious as well. Students can hardly wait to be in their presence, and they perform some monumental tasks, sometimes against monumental odds, to gain the master's approval. As students catch the fever, they become increasingly demanding of themselves. If they love birds, then they have to understand the ecology that surrounds their feathered friends. They are not satisfied with the obvious solution because they know it comes too easily. So they continue to explore. They want answers that cause new paths of thought and explanation. They want to invent new machines. They want to become the prominent names in their fields. If a teacher can stimulate that kind of energy, desire, and enthusiasm in students, he or she has to be considered great.

Third, great teachers have exceptional skill in motivating people. They have the charisma to cause others to take risks and challenges they never dreamed possible. They build confidence in others to plunge onward in new arenas and to accept no less than the best. Their skills become most apparent when student efforts and confidence lag, when there seems to be no way to solve the problem, and they carefully regenerate confidence, energy, and drive. They send the budding knights back to the dragons and in search of the Holy Grail.

Finally, they are selfless people who know they are making themselves obsolete by creating a new generation of the brightest and the best who will ultimately outshine them. It is the way with teaching. The satisfaction comes from watching the new talent and passion headed toward their worlds to be conquered. That is what great teachers do.

Average Teachers

If we examine any organization, we'll find that the bulk of the participants do their duties at average levels of performance. They are given tasks and the parameters in which to perform them. They rarely look beyond the limits of the assignment to see a bigger picture, and they almost never take risks. They do their jobs competently but never seek to go beyond. Maybe they live by these limitations because they feel little hope or interest in improving their organizations. They want job security, and they want to be liked.

The educational world at all levels is filled with average teachers. School systems depend on them because they come to work on time, care about their work, and rock no boats. The problem with them is that they have no passion to push the limits, to put in the extra time and effort to improve the systems in which they work. They take the syllabus, texts, or programs, develop safe lesson plans, and make uninspired presentations to students who get bored. They depend too much on worksheets designed in publishing mills with virtually no contact with students. Without the teacher's manuals, they would be in deep trouble because they don't want to expend their own creativity looking at the material.

Yet most of these teachers are thoroughly decent people who care about their students—to a point. They like their jobs because there is the security of tenure and a long summer break. Furthermore, few systems demand much beyond average from them, and they feel safe working with quite attractive people like them. Because they rock no boats, their administrators also feel safe in knowing what to expect from them. After all, many of those administrators came from the ranks of average teachers.

The problem comes when the community realizes that students are not being pushed hard, and the resulting educational achievement is average or worse. All of a sudden, community leaders wonder why many younger members of the local workforce lack the qualifications necessary to do jobs in their plants. They discover that the dropout rate in the community is way too high because the poorer students are not receiving the support and instruction they need to be successful. Admission pools to colleges dry up when the graduates of institutions do not gain admission to the desired graduate programs or get offers of employment from good companies. Average instruction leads to boredom in the classroom and poor results.

If we accept the premise that a good education for all students is a really important goal for the community, why do we allow our classrooms to be led by average teachers who do not inspire students? The answer, I think, is that we are too kind. We don't want to hurt people by pushing them. We know the average soul has a family to raise and bills to pay. We see these people regularly at church or at the grocery store. We see them as our neighbors, and we like them. But mediocrity brings mediocrity.

We have to motivate the average teacher to become a good teacher. Sure, programs to do so have been put in place. Most teachers attend in-service workshops or summer sessions at colleges and universities to maintain their credentials. Yet the average teacher participates partially by only going through the motion while there, and he or she puts up with completing the task. Furthermore, many of the sessions they attend are pretty dreadful themselves in that they offer little or no challenge to the attendee. They are designed to be painless means to fulfill requirements. We have to create atmospheres in our educational world that demand the average either become superior or leave. Yes, there are teacher evaluations in place to assess and advise, but too often there is not enough desire in the average teacher to change the status quo. Change is difficult, but it is constantly with us, and it makes us better if we react properly to the stimulus. Those who refuse to respond to change must be left behind.

But in too many academic institutions, we make it easy for the average to become firmly entrenched. Not only do we not challenge them, we have tenure, which virtually guarantees adequate teachers and administrators a job for their whole careers. Tenure came about to protect teachers from being arbitrarily fired for no good reason. Its time has come and gone in this country. Federal laws protect all workers to some degree. Why should academia have protections found nowhere else in the workplace? Why shouldn't all teachers face regular evaluation and consequences for doing an average or poor job? Why should people get pay raises for longevity in a job rather than merit? In light of the savage economic times we have just witnessed, no one who works in the free market system should tolerate systems that protect the average.

Not long ago I read *Jack: Straight from the Gut* by Jack Welch, who transformed General Electric Corporation. He realized that the company needed to develop a culture of excellence if it were to survive and thrive. One of the tools he used in doing that was to have each manager annually rate his employee as top 10 percent, average, and bottom 10 percent. The top group received serious pay incentives; the average group gained mediocre financial reward; the third group was terminated. This policy affected every level of the organization from top to bottom. Implementation of this policy became very difficult for managers after the third year because more and more of the members of the average group fell to the third group and disappeared. The managers had to cut loose people they liked, and such was painful. Yet the company's performance grew dramatically as did its profits and worldwide stature. Sure, the program was cutthroat, but the results brought excellence and reward for the strong employees. If academia were to implement a similar program, each child in the schools would benefit. So would the reputations of the school system in the community.

It is time for us to stop rewarding mediocrity in the schools. We would do everyone, including the average teacher, a favor by demanding excellence. The surviving teachers would become re-energized, and the others would find a workplace better suited for them. They would probably gain greater self-respect knowing that they were in occupations they liked a whole lot better. Students would receive better challenges in the classroom and grow faster from the experience. If industry can remake itself, so can academia. There is no room for the average in classrooms where our children, our finest resource, are trained for the future.

Bad Teachers

Too many schools have bad teachers. School districts, especially those with swelling enrollments, get desperate to fill vacancies just before a year begins, and they sometimes make poor hiring decisions. Also, some members of the staff lose energy and incentive necessary to be good teachers. Sometimes health issues intervene. In any case, bad teachers must be purged.

The worst set of bad teachers is those who prey upon students with malice aforethought. These are abusers. They have range from the worst case of physical molester to the mental abuser—one who harms students with belittling barbs. The intention in both cases is to maim and destroy. Any instance of such behavior ought to result in immediate termination and prosecution if appropriate. Yet many of these people remain on faculties and staffs for years, harming multi-generations of students.

A second group is comprised of those who accepted a position simply to make a living. They have no interest in educating. They take up space and do nothing positive for students as their motivation is simply personal. The ease by which a person can gain job security with good benefits attracts too many lazy people who do not care about students. They want only a soft, cushy job for themselves.

A third group is the most difficult to deal with because they are a product of the educational system. These are the worn-out, long-term teachers who have put in their time waiting to reach the magic age of retirement. Miss Failure and many others lie here. They are financially trapped in this position because over the years of teaching service, they have not had the opportunity to build the financial base to extricate themselves from working every day. So they go to class with the sole motivation of surviving another day and, thus, getting closer to the golden parachute. They lack the energy to motivate themselves much less the students. This group grows annually, and right now it is growing rapidly as the baby boomers age out, thus putting a huge teacher shortage strain on communities. We have to find ways to use these older people productively outside the classroom, allowing them to reach their pension programs safely, but do it in such a way as to not lose face. If doing so is an economic impossibility, then we have to bite the bullet and otherwise get these people out of the classrooms.

The world our children face is going to present increasingly tough competitions, and we must do whatever we can to prepare them for that. Providing the best, not worst, teachers is a huge step in that direction. Jack Welch would not spare these people in his world; nor should we in ours.

Students

They come in all shapes, sizes, abilities, and interest levels, but they have a common denominator. **Each is the most important person in any classroom**. They are, directly or indirectly, the paying customers who give schools and teachers the reason to exist. Too often teachers and administrators forget this fact as they focus on their own concerns rather than the important one: the education of the student.

Nevertheless, each student is vitally important in the school. Educators have to remember that as we go about our business. Each student deserves constant respect until he or she proves unworthy of it. Each, to some degree, has a fear of what's to come and of his or her ability to accomplish the necessary tasks to complete the goals. Educators need to minimize those fears and support the efforts. Our job is to nurture and strengthen our students in the learning process. We should not expect or allow failure in our realms because ultimately we fail each time our students do. Furthermore, we fail our community and disavow the trust given to us by that community.

People wonder about the troublemakers or passive-aggressive students who refuse to learn. With very few exceptions, we have created them. We, the teachers, have allowed them to fail by not paying enough attention to them. The little child coming to kindergarten from an impoverished, broken home has needs not found in a classmate from a situation where he or she has had all sorts of attention and comfort. It's a school's job to bring the weaker students to the level of the others. At the same time, it is the responsibility of all parents, no matter what their economic status, to prepare their children for school. The classroom is not a vacuum apart from the community. It is an important part of it.

The first step in that process is getting students to trust the teacher and to want to be successful. Instructors have to treat them with respect and kindness. We have to show them that we like them as people. We have to demonstrate that we care. It is far easier to get people to do what we want when they know we are all working together in a positive way. There is no place in the classroom for remarks that are detrimental or otherwise harmful to the student. Those hurtful words can cause deep injury to the psyche and stop the learning process. In fact, they are sometimes carried for life. One nagging fear I have about my long teaching career is how many students I might have harmed early with sarcastic remarks that hurt when they were meant to be funny. I hope there were few if any. No worthwhile relationship can be built on a lack of trust, and no trust can be built when one party in question commits harmful acts to the other. I have encountered educators who deliberately beat up on students to make themselves look good. Those people have always angered me because they are preying on defenseless students, who are dependent upon them for a grade.

Students have questions about the work they are doing. Sometimes they ask because they don't understand. Sometimes they ask because they are excited about a concept and want to learn more. Sometimes they simply want recognition. All are valid reasons, and educators have to respond with sensitivity to those questions to continue the student's intellectual growth. Sometimes when there are no questions, there is little or no learning going on. Test or other assessments should be positive exercises. While these exercises ask students to demonstrate their knowledge, they should be fair and expected. They should be the students' chance to strut their stuff and feel good about the tasks and material learned.

Students sometimes become lost because they've become unfocussed. If we are to lead students to successful learning, we have to lay out the prescribed path and make sure they don't wander off it. We have to accomplish this task with respect.

All of us operate more successfully when we know what's expected of us. We want to know what the rules are and what will happen to us when we do not live up to them. We also want to know the standards by which we are being judged. That's why teachers give out class rules and syllabi. We need to give clear assignments and define standards of measurement. We have to give tests and papers that cover the material we have actually covered in class, and we must prepare students for those assignments. I have always felt that a student of mine who fails a test is my failure rather than the student's. A graded assignment should be a positive rather than negative experience for the student. Success breeds success. As student confidence grows, so too does the desire to become more accomplished. Creating that desire within each student is our mission. When we have accomplished this task, we have given each student the ultimate respect.

Students are very fair. They come to our classrooms with open minds about instructors. They initially show varying degrees of respect for the role of teacher, but they rather quickly develop a degree of respect for each based on their observations in the classroom. Each teacher has an individual style based on his personality, education, experience, creativity, and energy. Some put together effective styles while others don't have a clue. Experience has taught me that students base their respect on the teacher's fairness, respect of student, integrity, willingness to be an individual, and knowledge of the subject.

Deep down, all students want to succeed. Success breeds success, and people grow from it. They use it to reach for greater honor and reward. Everyone, even the weakest, has a sense of self, and it is the educator's path to help that grow, allowing the person to achieve better success and standing. That is our job.

Greatest Diversity in the World

The American educational system is amazingly diverse. Vast numbers of dollars, both public and private, are spent in the process of teaching people. We provide schooling for everyone who wants it, be they toddler, teen, adult, or senior citizen. Some schools are exclusive, but many are anything but. Governments of all levels provide funding for the public education viewed necessary for the country by founders Thomas Jefferson, John Adams, and others. Churches of many faiths spend contributed dollars to provide schooling from kindergarten through graduate studies. An increasing number of students are taught at home. Other organizations provide learning strictly to make a profit, and they survive and flourish when they perform their tasks well.

Our educational diversity is renowned all over the world, and students come from everywhere to study here. It is a light that draws eager learners, many of which return to their own country. The diversity of funding guarantees a variety of options, but there are organizations that rightfully monitor the quality of educational output of most schools. For example, most school and colleges are monitored by the National Association of Schools and Colleges or a regional sub-body. All states have many standards, which must be met by all schools, even homeschooling. Increasingly states are holding school personnel accountable for their work in class by having students take and pass year-end examinations. It is right that there be standards to which teaching and learning are measured because they guarantee a degree of equality and quality throughout the various delivering bodies.

The question of accountability presents a major rub. How do we go about making sure that schools do what they claim to do? Well, in the marketplace, we make those decisions with our dollars. We buy products we think are fairly priced and well made. We steer clear of people who cheat us or who do not perform well. In the educational system, it is harder to make the same choices. For example, the law demands that we send our children to school, and the government provides public schools for that purpose. Until the rise of charter schools, the local public school was the only inexpensive option available to most citizens. Yes, the wealthy could send their children to many private options, and many churches provide relatively inexpensive options for the followers of their faith. But most of us have had to send our kids to the local schools. Who would guarantee that those children would get a good product?

As pointed out earlier, local school boards, state and federal departments of education, and private accrediting organizations helped do that. However, in this country, most public schools fall short of any standards of excellence. Certainly, each year they send millions of graduates on to colleges, universities, technical schools, etc., where they succeed. But annually millions of students leave the same public schools without a diploma or success. They fall through many cracks and are lost. As a result, poverty and crime continue to grow. We lose too many of our young each year. Enrollment in the prison system and despair grow too fast in segments of our population. We have to change the way we do business.

The children of the haves stand a far better chance of success than do those of the have-nots because there are many more options available to them. Those toddlers are not hungry or scared. They are pampered, and they have all sorts of experiences that equip them well for school. With that head start, they are off and running before other children can catch up. Children attending schools in wealthy districts such as Westchester, New York, Hollywood, California, Chapel Hill, North Carolina, and other similar economic areas have teachers who are more experienced and better paid than those in school districts in deep rural or inner city districts. We all know that money talks. The haves get more of what they want, and the have-nots get what little they can. In this democratic country, we have to do better for those who struggle to do better.

Now don't get me wrong. Many have-nots are made of great stuff. They will not accept the status quo, and they will not allow their children to fall in the cracks. These people are used to fighting for what is theirs and more. They will not quit. At the same time, many of the haves are soft, and they think they should get the best because of who they are. Those fail, and they deserve to. It is absolutely vital to the health of our country that we change what we do in schools so that no children lose their way. George W. Bush's program No Child Left Behind was an attempt to do that. Unfortunately, it was underfunded and over-restricted to do that. It did, however, cause the public to question what went on in each classroom. It did rightfully heighten awareness of classroom accountability. But people focused too much on using simple test scores as the sole measure. We have to go back to the drawing boards.

Back to the subject of diversity. Immigration continues to change our population base and create significant problems in most classrooms. Not long ago I read an article in the *Charlotte Observer* that said more than one hundred languages were spoken by students in the Charlotte-Mecklenburg School District. Talk about difficulties for teachers, especially in classrooms of younger children! As the population diversity continues to grow, so do desires to have more and more cultural values built into the curricula. Couple diversity with poverty, which brings its awful pressure to schools, and the classroom problems increase by geometric proportions. This country has been and will continue to be the melting pot of cultures, and we have to create learning strategies that take this element of social change into consideration. It is a daunting task.

Over the past decade, school accountability has come to the forefront, especially in political discussion. There's lots of lip service to improving student output, especially test scores. Increasingly the business community wishes to compare those improved test scores with increased productivity and profitability in the world of free enterprise. Well, the business and educational systems don't operate under the same parameters. The raw material in the classrooms is not of singular measurable quality. Nor are the goals of all participants the same as they tend to be in business. Not all students respond to the same stimuli and rewards. They tend to be a little messier to corral and reach standards agreed upon by the ruling bodies. Nor do all parents want the same things for their children. Oh yes, according to headlines, strong morality in the classroom seems to be more important than it does in both the business and political communities.

Yes, we must agree to educate all the students in this country far better than we are doing now. We must gather our various talents and egos into a major focus on the educational needs of our students. We have to play that game rather than talk it. We have to find greater funding for schools. We have to demand that parents provide basic needs for their children, and we have to find ways to help those who cannot do so alone. We have to stop doing things like having a state legislature set calendar limits on school districts based on the demands of the tourist industry in the state. We have to have school administrators and teacher unions focus on what students need rather than what the adults in the program want. We have to bring the arts and physical education back to the schools, and we have to have schools cease being boring, irrelevant places for far too many of the students there. We must get rid of bad and average teachers, and we must produce and demand excellence for and of all the students. We must make the diversity of our students and our schools work together to help our country. When we do so, we will reenergize our country and make it once again the finest land in the world.

Poverty

In the spring of 2012, the people of the United States of America find themselves listening to the political rhetoric coming from candidates wishing to be elected. There has been too much focus on the needs of the wealthy and the middle class and too little on those impoverished. According to various sources, somewhere between 33 percent and 50 percent of our population live near or below the poverty line. Some school districts in every state are now feeding children three meals a day. Many districts feed all their children one or two meals a day. Growing numbers of kids are coming to school from homeless situations.

Poverty is running rampant in this country, "the land of the good and plenty." It is a factor that undermines efforts of teachers daily. How can youngsters learn when their whole attention is focused on basic issues of hunger, need, and fear? Maslow's hierarchy of needs tells us that learning anything is almost impossible if attention is focused on the most basic needs. Kids who come from worlds of nothing have little experiential background preparing them for the social and intellectual demands found in schools. Poverty forces parents to scrounge for absolute basic needs and, thus, not be able to provide emotional or intellectual needs for themselves much less their children. The resulting despair found among the impoverished robs most of the incentives for success found among those of us who have had more. It also feeds their need to make the quick, illegal buck or find artificial means of escaping reality, thus making their plight even worse.

Furthermore, this rapidly expanding poverty takes huge economic toil on the rest of us. Some, for example, resent spending school funds for meals for hungry kids. We pay exorbitant amounts of tax dollars to house prisoners who have turned to crime in a world of hopelessness and despair. We pay high medical bills to cover the costs of those who go to the emergency room for medical service because they have no other place to go. We pay higher prices to cover that cost of goods stolen daily by those truly in need. And I could go on and on with more examples.

We with some economic clout do our best to forget about those in need. They become invisible in our daily lives. One side of the current political debate cries for the needs of the 1 percent, in other words, how they should hold on to their money. The other side talks about the need to protect the middle class, which is disappearing. Both sides have valid arguments for their constituencies, but so does the remaining, and growing, group: the poor. Not since Lynden Johnson's war on poverty has there been a concerted national effort to ease the harm of poverty. In 2012, we have an economic world similar to that of the 1880s and 1890s: one in which the super-rich either lord over or ignore the rest. Yes, there are foundations and other philanthropic organizations trying to help, but there needs to be a national effort to help. We have to find ways in a positive manner allowing the downtrodden dignified ways to escape their hopeless plight. Welfare programs as they presently exist do not do so. We have to redesign programs so that they provide aid without robbing the recipients of dignity or giving them a sense of entitlement. Demanding work for aid does that. Look to the success of Habitat for Humanity. That program has provided housing for many of the needy, but it does so in a way that demands effort and financial input from the recipient. It gives dignity to people who need it. The program has had a further benefit of rebuilding poor neighborhoods and building a broad sense of community between the volunteers and the needy. FDR faced a similar plight in the 1930s, and he brought creative thought to the government. We must have a rebirth of positive, creative energy in Washington now, but hope for it looks dim.

If we do not redesign our current economic world, poverty will get us all, even the top 1 percent. It is a pervasive problem that can topple the best. When the down-trodden get angry, they tend to become violent. Look at the French Revolution. Look what happened in the '60's in this country. Watts, Detroit, and Washington, DC felt the wrath of the poor. We must work together to avoid repeat performances of this ilk. Futhermore, we must work to unite our people rather than increasing economic divides that harm many, especially children.

Changing an Attitude

One of the biggest and most important issues facing public education is that a significant segment of the population does not believe in it. Once upon a time, parents sent their children to school with a confidence that they would learn and be prepared for the future. Now too many view time spent in public schools with skepticism and lack of respect. Their own experiences there helped build this attitude, and a general world-weariness heaps fuel on that fire. Corporate leaders have voiced opinion that the public schools don't produce students who have the ability to do tasks their businesses need to have done. Many of the very wealthy have for years spent vast amounts of money educating their children at private institutions. Private schools of all sorts are rapidly appearing all over the country, and the question of charter schools has been, and still is, a political football. Finally, homeschooling is a practice on the rise.

The first change schools must make is to show communities that they are serious, professional institutions working as hard as possible for the benefit of the students going there. They have to reach out to the parents and seek their opinions and help. They have to send students home every day with a sense of accomplishment and a commitment to continue their striving diligently the next day. There is nothing new about this concept. Many of us remember the movie from the '80s about the calculus teacher in a low-income school in Los

Angeles who taught students a very tough math course successfully by convincing them they could do the work. He then demanded they do it. When the successful AP scores came in, everyone in the community believed.

Schools have to convince each parent that each child is the most important person in the school. Teachers have to have strong contact with the home. They have to relay student victories as well as the defeats. They have to invite the community to see what students accomplish. I have been to several grandparents' days at various elementary schools. The rooms are always crowded with adults and students mixing well. Kids like to show off their skills, and doting parents and grandparents want to see those victories. So too with PTA meetings. All these events bring a bonding between school and family. They have to continue beyond the first few grades into middle and high schools.

Schools are academic places first. Therefore, they have to convince the community that academic victories are more important than athletic ones. In far too many academic institutions, the athletic tail wags the academic dog, and the wrong values are passed on. Look at the scandals coming out of the athletic worlds of many of our major universities. They are shameful. And while a few coaches or administrators may lose jobs, etc., the message comes loud and clear that athletics is the most important part of the universities. Money rules, and unfortunately, money has a way of corrupting what is good. I admire the Ivy League and Division III schools, which keep athletics as a less important part of their program. They see themselves as academic places first. High schools need to do the same. So do elementary schools.

Teachers have to show their communities that they are serious professionals out to work hard to have their students excel. They need to be professional in every sense of the word. They have to work hard. They need to dress the part. They need to walk the walk as well as talk the talk. They are role models every day, and they cannot forget that.

School administrators have to make sure that schools are attractive places where students want to come every day. Doing so means caring for the facility so it is clean and attractive, but it also means that it is a place where activity and good humor hum steadily. They have to treat their staffs with respect and demand only the best. They cannot coddle the mediocre or incompetent. They have to present achievable goals that lift the effort level and spirits of all. They have to push. They have to support. They have to seek dreams from all and help fulfill them. They have to build good teams. To do all these tasks, they have to have freedom from strong, meddling control at the bureaucratic top. In few cases does the trickle down theory work. The most effective changes come from those underlings who understand how to improve their performances and make their institutions better. When workers have the opportunity and need to improve their workplace, synergism develops, and everybody wins.

Old ways of instruction have to disappear because they are obsolete. The Internet offers opportunities for learning that were never available to us as we went through school, and the information on it rarely becomes obsolete. Textbooks do. They are also hideously expensive, and they get shabby after a few years of service. There is not a school in the country that does not have a store of useless old books that may turn students off. The school district that my older two grandchildren attend spends its textbook money on laptop computers for students. They then access the Internet, with its almost infinite resources, at their fingertips. Student research is current, and they can put together imaginative, creative projects that really interest and challenge them and others.

Another really neat tool the computer brings to the classroom is that the teacher can much better track the achievement of the student and individualize instruction to best fit the needs of the student. Wow! If the teacher really knows what he or she is doing, she can be sure that each child is reaching and fulfilling potential. Individual programs of research can stretch imaginations and talents far more than those awful, old workbook things we used to do in classrooms. Here is a technical tool that can implement the good aspects of George Bush's No Child Left Behind. Students like to use electronic gadgets, and they are far more likely to do homework if they can do it on machines.

The college I work for is working toward becoming a paperless institution. Information can readily be passed by students to instructors in paperless forms. The work can be processed by instructors and returned without being converted to paper. Records are kept electronically, etc. The library spends money purchasing current subscriptions to information on the Internet rather than buying paper journals that take up space and are less accessible to students. Technology has given teachers better ways to do our jobs, and we must use it to give students the best opportunity to be prepared for their adult world.

Going back to a point I made earlier, many parents have little or no respect for school because they themselves had bad experiences there. Therefore, they do not support schools now. Yet parents are won over when their kids get excited about things. Think of the soccer moms who hated soccer until their little ones got involved. Then the moms really got into the programs, and soccer fields appeared all over the country. Well, the schools are here, but they need the same support. All we have to do is get the moms and dads there to support and help. Thankfully, there are parents who support school activities, but we need more. I am reminded of an example found in Charlotte, North Carolina in the 1970's. The Supreme Court mandated busing of students across the district to achieve the same racial balance in each school that was found in the community at large. The city handled this social upheaval with honor and effort. When a significant number of white students were bussed from the then finest high school in the city to a different school in the poor black district, the parents decided to make the new school of their students the best in the city. They became a very active PTA. They raised money. They demanded appropriately that the academic performance be improved to meet the needs of their students. They supported the already strong athletic and musical programs. In short, they became deeply involved in the life blood of that school, and it became a show place in the community. Other school districts have similar stories. Strong, positive parental involvement brings about improved school performance and pride. Everybody wins.

We have to look at the ways we fund schools and the way the monies are expended, but we have to do so in ways that are creative and controllable. Fiscal responsibility has to be a cornerstone of whatever changes educational institutions make. Our leaders have to be good but forward-looking stewards. The skyrocketing costs of education cannot continue at the rates at which they have. The major problem with those costs is that they are dominated by teacher salaries, which are certainly not princely now. Thus, the question arises, how can we make teachers more productive without breaking the community? How can we attract new talent to the schools unless we offer competitive financial packages? How can the computer help institutions serve students better and reduce costs? All these issues are currently being examined, but we have to continue doing so with creativity and with a sense of improving rather than cutting. These questions are hugely complex and will take talented people to solve them.

Success breeds success. It also builds bandwagons and enthusiasm. We need to focus on the needs of each student and develop our schools so they really benefit everyone. Dropout rates have to become figures of history rather than reality. Academic programs have to provide students with necessary life skills so they can compete in a rapidly changing world.

Finis

As I look toward the future, I remain very optimistic. I see recognition that our process of educating has flaws and issues that are being identified and can be fixed. I see a history of strong people in this country who are adaptable and who can make dreams realities. The space race showed that. So did our movement toward fulfilling Martin Luther King Jr.'s dream. We still have a long way to go on that one, but we have made substantial progress. I see many dedicated students who know they can succeed, and I see young teachers and administrators with determination and dreams in their hearts. I see a fairness and willingness to pitch in and help among our people. I see creativity and humor alive and well in our land. I guess we old-timers did some things right.

Part III

Addendum

Preface to the Addendum

Much of the writing I have done has come directly from my experience in the classroom. It seems appropriate to give a sampling of pieces I have created over the years because many were started or edited while students worked on their own projects in computer labs. One in particular, "Fenninger's Four Laws of Writing," was developed over many years of teaching composition and reading the works of master writing teachers such as Strunk and White, William Zinsser, and many others. "Professional Statement" I wrote on an application for full-time employment at Mitchell Community College. Three pieces—"Reflections on Heroes," "Josephine," and "Solitude"—were written as models for essay topics I assigned. "Herb Smedley" came as the result of an incident I encountered in a classroom. The poetry came in bits and pieces over the years, and I think it reflects my growth as a writer. So enjoy.

Reflections on Heroes

This essay was written in the spring of 2012. It was meant to be an example of an essay which reflects upon a subject in a sort of stream of consciousness approach. The class consisted of many students who had walked far more difficult paths than I had, and I became impressed, even awed, by their dedication to self-improvement. My hat is off to them.

Heroic behavior is a quality we all learn early. There are national heroes like the presidents or famous leaders who rise above the ordinary and gain timeless recognition. Everyone knows who George Washington is. Martin Luther King Jr. and Jackie Robinson are known worldwide. Princess Diana had her moment in fame and will be mourned for generations. Superman and Batman live on into new generations, and Paris and Achilles have been fighting for thousands of years. Kobe Bryant, Tim Tebow, Joe DiMaggio, Peyton Manning, and countless other sports figures make the record books and gain momentary heroic status. We all are better for their efforts as they make us happy and cause us to reach for new heights. It's comforting to know that the mighty are out there struggling and fighting hard ultimately in our behalf.

Yet heroic efforts come not from a desire to gain notoriety but from a need to do something for the right reason. True heroes are frequently not known. For example, while George Washington is heralded for crossing the Delaware and beating the Hessians on Christmas Eve, he would never have done so without the cold, tired guys who rowed the boats and actually fought in the snow. Martin Luther King Jr. was, and still is, an inspiration to many, many people, but he never would have gained his fame without the brave souls who at his behest rebelled nonviolently and were injured or killed. President Kennedy's insistence that we beat the Russians in putting a man on the moon would never have happened without thousands of faceless people working to accomplish a goal. Most goals would never be reached if it were not for unsung souls putting forth effort to make things happen. Churches wouldn't raise money, and local fire companies would wonder where their new equipment might come from.

Yet the big names get the fame, and far too frequently they tarnish it. Many too many famous people fall because of their own misbehavior. Too many major politicians are caught in scandalous behaviors that bring about their downfalls. Too many sports figures and artists cause their own ruin by turning to drugs, alcohol, or some other ruinous way of life. They frequently fall through their own stupidity and greed. Maybe that's why those with integrity and honor stand out in history.

When I was a boy, my heroes were Richie Ashburn and Robin Roberts of the Philadelphia Phillies. Both were great players on mediocre to bad teams, but they were stars who are enshrined in the Baseball Hall of Fame. I wanted to be both players, of course, because then baseball was my life. Well, I never could hit very well, and throwing unhittable strikes was an impossible task for me. Those men are still heroic figures in my life, but I have found far more important ones.

Most of my students are my heroes. While I have no use for those who attend class only to collect financial aid and do no work whatsoever, I have infinite respect and patience for those who are there with a seriousness of purpose. They are unquestionably the most important people in the room.

They come from all walks of life, but far too many share a common experience of being hammered by something or someone. Many have suffered from all sorts of abuse. Some have fought poverty and illness. Others have faced tough defeats. Some have returned to school after being away for many years, and they find the task daunting. Many are single parents doing their best to provide for their children and work to improve their lot in life. All are tireless, as they both work and attend school and do whatever else they have to do. All are striving hard to gain the skills and credentials necessary to improve their lives. All have dreams to reach. All have the urge to learn, a sense of humor, and a rightful sense of pride. All welcome kind words and gentle laughter.

My heroes come to school with dignity, integrity, and pride, and they try their damndest to learn how to write good essays or to figure out how stories and poems work. They bring their experiences to the papers and discussions, and we all come out of the interchanges better students. My heroes demand that I take them seriously and teach to the best of my ability. They do so, not unpleasantly, but with a challenge to give them insights I may have that will help them solve increasingly more complex verbal problems. I willingly accept their challenge.

We are all a part of the human experience. Some have and must struggle harder than others at certain skills, but then, none of us is good at everything. As we bring our efforts to class and grow from the interaction, then we accomplish goals sometimes not expected. We develop liking and respect for one another as well as the increasing ability to solve word problems. Isn't that what an educational institution should do?

So, real heroes are frequently those who make us better people and workers. They are people who don't let us down by being monstrous hypocrites. They are those who quietly leave a mark on us as we march along our paths, trying to do the right things. So I thank you, my heroes, for giving me the urge to teach more effectively and to be sure no one leaves the course unsuccessfully.

Fenninger's Four Laws of Writing

I. Convince the reader.

This rule is the essence of building good essays, and there are several parts.

1. Be certain that the organization of the paper is clear, concise, and properly ordered.
    a. Be sure the introduction grabs the reader's attention and that the thesis statement is clear.
    b. Be sure the plan of development is clear and properly ordered.
    c. Be sure that the developmental paragraphs are convincing and in the same order as the elements presented in the plan of attack.
2. Be certain that there are no holes in the logical pattern. The argument needs to be sound and on target. Avoid getting off topic.
3. Be sure conclusions are properly set up and developed. No conclusion is valid unless it is adequately supported by logic or sources, either primary or secondary.
4. Further note on sources: When writing about literature, there is no better source than the author's own words from the text

to support a claim. Secondary sources cited must be valid and timely. No source without an accountable foundation is valid in scholarly work; hence, as a source, *Wikipedia* is valueless.

5. The author of an academic paper has the total responsibility for using legitimate source material and citing them properly. There is no excuse for failure in this area.

6. Be sure that the tone and language usage and construction are proper for the assignment. Nothing convinces a reader more of a student's skill and seriousness of purpose than effective use of language.

II. **Use the precise word.**

The English language contains over six hundred thousand words, allowing writers the greatest word choice of any language. Choose for meaning. For example, *plod* does not mean the same as *scamper.* Use the word that best fits. Give specific details. Don't say the man has coins in his pockets. Instead maybe Herb Smedley has quarters clanking in his pockets as he walks.

There is a corollary to this rule: If given the choice between a long, sophisticated word or a common, shorter word, select the latter. But if the former best fits the situation, use it. In any case, we always want to select words known by the reader to avoid his or her confusion.

Whenever possible, use active rather than passive verbs. They create more clout and create shorter sentences.

A sophisticated aspect of this rule is to make the vocabulary choice fit the subject and the tone of the essay. If the piece is formal, then so must the tone be. Ultimately, we want each word to develop the idea presented in the thesis statement.

III. **Say the most about the subject using the fewest words.**

Deliver the message totally without clutter and confusion. Understand that every word presents the possibility of creating an error. Therefore, eliminate words not needed. Look at sentence constructions with the thought of simplifying or reducing them. Can a clause be reduced to a phrase or a phrase to a word? Asking this sort of question leads to elimination of clutter. Clarity of thought usually comes without clutter. The practice of this law comes in two phases of the writing process: the creation of the draft and the editing of the essay before the final copy. In *Hamlet,* Polonius ironically says, "Brevity is the soul of wit." Unfortunately, he is unable to live by his own words. We must try to do so when writing to avoid clutter and to impress. Yet in carrying out this task, we must never omit thoughts and details vital to the argument. We need to take care that we prune well.

IV. **Be anything but ordinary.**

Our task in writing academic papers is to present a subject in such a manner that the instructor is convinced by the submitted paper that you are brilliant. Once he or she reaches this conclusion, a great grade is sure to follow.

1. Remember that you are not a boring person; therefore, it behooves you not to write a boring paper.

2. Pick a topic that's a little out of the ordinary but within the realm of the assignment. Readers of papers get bored reading about the same works or the tried-and-true topics. Take a chance on something a little different.

3. Create fresh ideas. Avoid trite phrases, symbols, arguments, etc. Remember that instructors have piles of papers to read, and they get numb after reading for a while. Think about doing something different that causes renewed interest rather than a deepening desire to have the pile disappear.

4. Polish your written expression and manuscript form so they shine well above the norm. Nothing else better demonstrates academic prowess.

5. Never forget to be yourself in your paper. The dominant voice must be yours. Any other raises unpleasant questions in the reader. Remember that a paper is an opportunity for you, the student, to strut your stuff. If you approach the assignment with a positive attitude rather than a defeatist one, you have a far greater chance to do well.

Professional Statement

I have spent the majority of my working career in education. Several times I ventured away from this field into other endeavors, but I keep coming back to the world I really enjoy: that of helping students gain proficiency in dealing with the English language and the interpretation of literature. Last year when I came to Mitchell Community College as a part-time instructor, I had no idea that I would enjoy teaching students here as much as I have. I have regained a sense of purpose and enjoyment from the experience, and I am confident that most of the students in my classes have enjoyed and benefited from their experience with me.

I believe that a healthy, vibrant educational process is vital to the continuing strength and success of our country and our people. I believe that the most important piece in that process is the development and continuance of colonies of teachers who believe in the positive growth of their students as people and as technicians of whatever skills they study. By showing respect for students as people and challenging them to increased academic demand, good teachers can bring those students to levels of skill and intellectual achievement beyond expectation. I also believe a hugely important element in student growth comes through a building of confidence within that student to tackle new challenges with the sense that the sky's the limit with proper effort and struggle. It is the teacher's responsibility to build that confidence, to demand effort, and to support the growth. Teachers are successful only if they work even harder and demand more of themselves than the students they teach.

My curriculum vitae demonstrates my varied, accomplished background and creative search for intellectual and professional growth. I maintain the vitality I've had over the years by striving to teach every class well and writing poetry on the side. My instructional load at Mitchell is almost that of a full-time instructor; therefore, the small additional load would not be overly burdensome. I am willing to commit to a three-year segment, at the whim of the college of course. I feel as though I have found a home here and wish to contribute as much as I can.

Josephine

Josephine was our cat when I was a boy. Sort of nondescript gray, she was, nonetheless, attractive enough to give birth to approximately 129 kittens before she died. One could say she was a bit promiscuous. In any case, despite our mother's denials, she ruled the house.

My uncle Scott was a career officer in the US Army. In the early '50s he received orders to spend three years in Iran, and his family could not take their pets. As a result, we inherited Mac, very large, mostly German shepherd. Mac's first action upon arrival was to chase Josephine up the mulberry tree. He felt proud of himself until Josephine decided to retaliate. When he was not looking, she jumped on his back, claws out, and rode the screaming dog around the yard. It did not take the long for the two to have mutual respect and become fast friends.

On day Josephine got very sick. She lay under some bushes while her litter (there was always a litter!) was stuck in the basement. She could not get to the hungry kittens to nurse them. Mac somehow understood the predicament and knew he needed to help. He went to the kittens, picked up each by the head, and carried them unharmed to Josephine. My mother saw him doing so and feared that he was killing the kittens, but she watched and understood what was happening. Those tiny kittens certainly looked silly hanging out of Mac's mouth. They looked even sillier with soaking wet heads and totally dry bodies, but they nursed contentedly. They all grew up.

My mother became very good at convincing all sorts of people that they needed kittens. After all, she had much practice. Occasionally, however, she was not fast enough to Josephine's satisfaction in clearing a litter. But Josephine had skills in this area as well. When the time came, she would line up the little ones and take them for a hike through the neighborhood. When she reached a place she felt appropriate, she would turn on one kitten, forcing it to remain at its new home. Then she would march to her next stop, and then the next, etc., until all kittens had new digs. That left her free to start the cycle all over again.

I don't remember what ever happened to Josephine. She probably died of overproduction. In any case, she produced too many kittens, and Mac never harmed one.

Solitude

Sometimes everyone needs a comfortable place to be alone and contemplate the present state of affairs. Better than fifty years ago, when I was a boy growing up outside of Springtown, Pennsylvania, I could find solace sitting on the concrete slab covering one of the stone entry walls to the Haupt's Mill Covered Bridge. Very few came down the dirt road that disappeared into the bridge and reappeared at the other end. Mr. McPeak, the mailman, drove through daily about eleven thirty, and the Browns, who lived just up the hill, travelled through several times a day. The Boys, who lived farther up the hill, also occasionally wandered along. There weren't many other wayfarers on this deserted road. Somehow while sitting alone, I found comfort from the textures of the concrete seat and weathered boards of the bridge when I really needed it. Maybe the burbling of Cook's Creek under the bridge added to the peace.

I went there for regrouping when I needed to, especially right after I had sinned mightily or report cards had just come out. My mother, who was rarely pleased with my lack of academic progress, was remarkably successful in relaying her opinions of my shortcomings. Frequently I had to rebuild resolve to continue fighting along my academic path and becoming a better person and son. Twenty minutes by myself or with the dogs splashing around in the creek made a great difference. The silence and gentleness of the woods and the sense of history emanating from a relic of times gone by urged me to not give up and reassured me that things would turn out all right. It's too bad that some idiot later burned that beautiful bridge to the ground simply because he did not want anyone passing his house. I understand his desire for isolation but am saddened because the bridge is gone and the county road that went through it is now a dead-end private lane with No Trespassing signs. But of course, now, that whole world is long gone, and so is my childhood with its insecurities.

Yet even as we age, we need a place to seek solitude and a chance to take a deep breath, thus recharging our batteries. We all find those places somewhere and are better off with the discovery. A little time alone gives us time to reflect and then plan on dealing with daily stresses and becoming healthier people. Today I have a wonderful piece of ground on Childers Road in Rowan County. It's quiet, and I can piddle around harmlessly. Sometimes there are neighbors wanting to chat, and sometimes there are chores to be done, but sometimes, there are times when the hammock calls.

I'll never forget that bridge even though it's long gone. Nor will I forget the farm when I can no longer go there. But I'll bet that even when I'm in a wheelchair, I'll find a private space.

Herb Smedley

Herb Smedley sat stunned. After reading about twenty-five thousand papers over twenty-five or so years, this was the first time he had encountered a problem like this one. Oh sure, there had been issues of plagiarism, but never one of blatant paper duplication. One paper told of a young man at the beach who had put his wallet on the roof of his car while opening the car door. He had driven off, losing his wallet. Miraculously, the local sheriff called the man's grandfather, and the wallet was recovered that afternoon. Of course, the money inside was gone. The second variation of the same theme had a man in the mountains lose his wallet the same way. In that case, the sheriff had called the man's aunt, and the wallet, sans money, had been recovered. Equally miraculously, both stories had the exact same grievous mechanical error in the first sentence of the second paragraph. Herb had never seen such egregious plagiarism.

Disturbed for several reasons, Herb knew he had a serious problem on his hands. After all, he had just begun teaching his first class at a new place, and he had no idea how the department head or dean might want him to handle this matter. Furthermore, he was coming back to teaching after a fifteen-year hiatus, and he had not felt his normal teaching rhythm. Yet this situation really stuck in his craw. The stupidity of the action appalled him as did the total disregard for integrity on the part of the miscreants. He knew he had to meet with the students, explore the options, and find a solution that made sense for all parties.

Herb began to do his homework. First, he examined the school policy as stated in the course syllabus about academic dishonesty. He started there because he had given each student a copy of that policy and had discussed it in the first class. Then he pondered his options, of which there seemed to be several in handling the case. For example, Herb could counsel the students, fail the paper, report the students to the dean, or even suggest they be dropped from school for academic dishonesty.

While Herb's righteous voice of integrity screamed for him to have these perpetrators of dastardly deeds expelled, the teacher side cautioned against such strong action. That voice reasoned that the best lessons we learn come from our missteps and failures. While this debate raged mightily within his psyche, Herb ultimately decided to see how the students in question reacted to his meeting with them.

Herb copied each paper and attached one person's to the back of each other's. At the end of class, Herb asked both students to meet with him. The three sat at a round table outside the building, and Herb returned the two papers, which had no grade. He then asked both if they noticed that the paper being returned was thicker than those turned in. Both students said yes, and then Herb asked them to turn to page three and read. There was a strangled silence as both students discovered what Herb had found. Then there were some sputtering denials, which Herb quickly cut off. He told them that he could see three possibilities for the marked similarities of the papers. (1) One student had written the paper and given it to the other, who had made minor changes. Herb suggested that this was a poor possibility because he didn't think they were stupid enough to try that in class of only twenty-two students. (2) Both students had gone to the Internet seeking a short narrative, thus fulfilling the assignment. By bad luck, they had reached the same source, chose the same selection, and made almost no changes. (3) The poetic muses had struck both students with the same inspiration at the same moment. Herb allowed as though that was not a strong possibility. As the miscreants sat in stunned silence, Herb continued.

"There is clear collusion between you on this assignment. I have several choices before me in handling this matter. For example, I could issue a failing grade for the course. I could take the matter before the college dean, who could dismiss you from school and have your transcripts marked in such a way that you would have difficulty in gaining admission at any other school. Or I can handle the matter another way. I do not believe in failure. I believe in learning from our mistakes. I do not desire to add extra burden on lives in difficult times, but I do think integrity is the most important value we have. Therefore, as of now, you both have failing grades on this paper. You may rewrite them according to my rewrite policy and have the grade replaced. If you do, they had better look very different. Should there be a second instance of this academic dishonesty, I will slit your academic throats and feel good about doing it. I have nothing further to say on the subject. If you want to sit here and discuss the matter further, you may. I'm going home to have dinner."

Twenty-four hours later, the first rewrite appeared. The second came about a week later. There were no further problems, and both students passed the course. After the solution, Herb discussed the case with his department head, who felt the matter had been handled well. In retrospect, Herb felt good about the whole incident because the issue had been addressed, the students seemed to learn, and there were no repeats. Furthermore, the solution appealed to his sense of teaching—that students learn from correcting mistakes in an atmosphere where they are respected as people.

Little Things

Little things make our day:
Thanks for a job well done,
Satisfaction from helping someone,
Monarch butterflies flitting, feeding,
Happy laughter rolling through space.
Then that little touch from one who cares,
Even if it leaves sticky fingerprints.
Spirits lift; the day gets brighter.
We walk taller, happier.
How easily we can motivate
With soft word and caress.
Why do we wait too late?

February 2011

Starting Again

Here I go again.
Another section of English class
Beginning anew.
Sounds repetitious yet isn't.
Each group unique:
Different personalities,
Different skills,
Different desires.
Like an actor on a stage,
I must make material precise and clear
To stimulate and urge.
Each student has
A separate journey,
Tangential to mine but
More important as
It's fresh and filled with future.
Confidence to be built,
Skills to be mastered,
Paths to be planned and trod,
Horizons to be conquered.
Our country's future is our young.
We old-timers must share experience
To build new foresight and talent,
Making us replaceable with those having
Wisdom, insights, and strength superior to ours.

Serenity

Serenity softens.

Waters wash.

Cleansings comfort.

The girl at the fountain

Quietly renews strength

By allowing soft, splashing droplets,

Slowly meandering down a mountain stream,

To trickle through her

Kind, tired fingers used to aid

Those less fortunate or able.

Jagged rocks round the waterfall

Contrast the gentle rebirth of spirit,

Enabling the sylph to continue her

Gentle touching of those in need.

The sculpture's craftsmanship brings

A loving vision to concrete reality.

From concept to clay to metal to assembly,

An idea takes a shape

That stuns, then comforts.

Creative vitality brings serenity,

Helping ease our own

Trials and tribulations.

Ideas pass wordlessly in the silent sculpture garden,

Impacting visitors never imagined by the artist.

A work designed to immortalize

A young lady accidentally taken

Reaches our soul,

Giving rest and rebirth.

The sculptor's tactile presentation

Of abstract desire

Causes impetus for written abstraction,

Continuing the serenity.

Creative circles evolve.

Abstraction, solid structure, abstraction,

Interlinking artistic efforts

Build chains binding creations

With cosmic demands for tranquility.

The constant continuum

Of energy comforts.

Serenity softens.

This poem has been written as a result of my very strong emotional response to a sculpture found in Brookgreen Gardens in Murrells Inlet, South Carolina. The piece, entitled Raphell, was created in 1983 by Bruno Lucchesi. It was acquired by Brookgreen Gardens in 2002.

Triggers

Triggers trip unexpectedly.
Caught in the boredom of the moment,
We're frequently and accidentally
Transported to other times and places,
Some kind, some not.

The comfortable past:
A little boy wearing a bus driver's hat
Drives silent, invisible riders
On kitchen chairs through the house
To imaginary destinations afar.
Sand in shoes brings Myrtle Beach
With the ocean battering or soothing
And a sunny crisping unwanted.
Ever sixteen, Dusty's always lusty,
And the Chevy's ever headed to the levee
While somewhere else Mama sings,
"Hush, little baby, don't you cry."
Snowflakes bring me to that hill behind the covered bridge
Where we sledded too fast and crashed.
A red '42 Farmall H, sixty years ago
The biggest, baddest tractor
I'd ever seen,
Snorted and strained through appointed tasks
Only to be retired to a dusty shed.

Errant random trips to the past

Ease endless ennui caused by

Empty, mandatory, and mindless sessions of the now.

The uncomfortable present:

Those triggers sometimes hurt, kill, and maim.

Man cannot cease fighting or

Feeding the young to the Gorgons of war.

The flower power of the '60s got lost,

Leaving us mired endlessly

In other nasty conflicts too far away.

Once again elders delight in war profits

Brought about by their endless jingoism and egotism

While young unfairly continue to bear the ultimate brunt.

"When will they learn? When will they ever learn?"

Politicians have forgotten they are supposed to help us,

The electorate, not kill us off or rip us off

To fill their own pockets.

Sustained greed has brought our current economic plight.

What nasty actions will be triggered by the results?

After continued joblessness, endless foreclosures, discomfort, and fear,

When will the latent anger arise and maul?

What will be the trigger?

Unknowns of the future:

In times of fear, anger, and despair,

Comfort's brought by little ones on the way.

Maybe they can trigger new solutions to old problems.

Maybe they can be better stewards of the earth and of our coffers.

Maybe they can find peace on earth.

Maybe their wisdom and strength

Will destroy the need for more nasty triggers.

But then, maybe this possibility is so remote

That trying to escape our inevitability,

We trigger ourselves

To the vague, happy land of our past.

Currents

Full of currents,

Dancing, humming, high energy

Seeking worthy outcomes, satisfaction of parental expectations,

These students, upwardly mobile products of the haves,

Sit, taking the PSAT.

A rite of passage.

A rite of passage? Of seasons.

Over generations, quick fingers lovingly pick

the tiny red and black orbs of currents

Destined to be cooked, crushed and

Filtered into jelly the homemade way.

A rite of passage?

Within these students, very near the surface,

Hormones hop, causing their own currents,

Strong and too frequently undisciplined.

Yet these bodies and their currents are bound tightly and hopefully

By almost puritanical drives and fears of affluent parents.

While in bodies less fortunate, the have-nots,

Currents zing boldly and irrepressively

Spring free,

Catching too many hungry thirteen-,

fourteen-, and fifteen-year-old girls.

Babies having babies—a rite of passage.

Right back into the circle of poverty go too many.

Angry societal swirls—a rite of passage?

Rightful and fruitful social unrest of the

'60s—marches toward civil rights—

Replaced by the march of a million (only far fewer) in the '90s.

In the second, what is sought:

Recognition, publicity, acceptance of irresponsibility, justification?

The jelly—a sustenance of the past—

Takes on new currents yet represents constancy.

Flavor, now probably fat and taste free, for the toast

No longer satisfies yet is praised for being safer.

A rite of passage to older people used to the

safety of corporate paternalism

Now becomes an increase of broken expected financial promises

Leading to a great life of comfortable retirement.

A rite of passage.

Too many of these uptight students taking

the test unquestionably dance to the

Dictates of ETS while too many irresponsible or hopeless others

Dance to the dictates of peer pressure—

Both frequently creating blind chaos of

the individual soul and spirit

And of an orderly society.

Rites of passage used to mean steps to

Adulthood, responsibility, stature, satisfaction.

Have too many currents, like those of Pandora's box,

Sprung too free and uncontrollable?

Control—a feared word.

Who has it?

Who wants it?

Lifelong tug of war between the haves and the have-nots.

Wherein lies respect?

Wherein lies humanity?

Currents: creativity—impulses for discoveries and growth.

Countries, jellies, ideas, social swirls, economic patterns.

Sometimes the opening of creativity leads to death.

Witness the malaise brought on by the mass media,

And then watch the members wash their

hands of guilt as they stir the pot.

Then the bigger gobble the small.

"Bigger is better."

Yet the mergers of giant corporations

Kill thousands upon thousands of jobs, careers, dreams.

Currents, pervasive, sometimes wildly strong,

Sometimes highly destructive,

Moving through the rites of passage

Into the future—whatever that is.

Merry Christmas

'Tis time to take pause
From our chaotic world,
With hectic routines and nasty strife.
'Tis tinsel time,
A wonderful time
Despite its own stresses with
Hurrying hassled men and women,
Striving for the perfect holiday
In a time of economic angst.

Stop! Rejoice!
Christ is born!
The living eternal promises delight and renew.
As does Santa, who heightens childhood
Excitement and joy.

Christmas is for all children,
One born long ago and
Those filled with wonder each year.
With them we laugh, enjoy, and hope.

And the lights, the symbolic lights,
Gaily driving away haunting darkness,
At least for a little while.
Long ago quiet candles in churches and homes,

Now frequently raucous, radiant displays
Brighten communities of families.

Families: the cornerstone of society,
Now too many lost from the traditional form
But with strength and love anyway.
Christmas pageantry heightens our happiness
And family togetherness.

Joyous music,
From ancient airs though Bach and Handel,
Pop and country, to Crosby and the Chipmunks,
Fills the air.
Some bring majesty, some pleasant nostalgia,
Others leave gnawing headaches:
But all fills the world with unique holiday sound.

For this is a time we are one with another,
Wishing for peace,
Striving to be better,
Enjoying one another.

"Merry Christmas," voices joy beyond
Daily rituals, dalliances, and
Beautiful religious meaning,
Uniting those from all walks
To a temporary, united peace.

So to all, with rousing spirit,
'Tis time I say,
Merry Christmas to all, and to all good night.

Magnetism

We came.

Music called, and we came

Into a farmhouse with a family room built

of materials from the land.

The fireplace wall, stone from side to side and top to bottom,

Dominated surrounding wooden flanks and the tall open space.

Hot apples, fresh bread, and oyster stew teased from the kitchen.

Music, good food, and fellowship brought warmth.

The Magnet carried his guitar and fiddle.

A banjo, bass, and another guitar could not resist the pull;

Nor could neighboring listeners.

Old friends and new acquaintances greeted and shied.

Long-term threads of conversation picked up,

And new ones cautiously joined the running tale.

Individual random picking began.

Suddenly separate sawings and pluckings became harmonic airs.

Bluegrass enveloped.

Old rhythms, known lyrics, favorite melodies filled the room.

The Magnate's guitar sang, demanding leadership and attention.

In time all players took turns leading and harmonizing,

But only at the whim of the Magnet.

Order ruled.

Music dominated; conversation quieted.

Another banjo and mandolin joined,

Adding complexity to the simple tunes.

The pulling force brought more listeners of all ages.

And the dogs came.

As the door opened, in and out they went,

Tails wagging, noses working.

They belonged.

Food appeared and disappeared, but the music never stopped.

Nor did the arrivals.

Nor did the conversation, stories, and gentle laughter.

Somehow the world grew smaller.

Suddenly there were no strangers.

The music seductively warmed.

Some danced.

All enjoyed, especially the musicians.

The Magnet disappeared into his playing,

But his talent dictated and demanded.

The others felt the pull and responded.

I was reminded of gatherings before:

Sunday dinner with children and grandchildren;

Small groups around battered pianos, singing Christmas carols

Or other well-known songs;

Circles around campfires listening to eerie

tales while toasting marshmallows;

Wedding guests throwing rice with love and laughter;

Sad hymn singers at the final resting place;

Summer picnickers saying grace before hot

dogs, ice cream, and fireworks.

People pulled together by a stronger force,

Finding warmth, belonging, and pleasure

In simple, good, basic gatherings.

Worldly sophistications complicate and confuse.

Warp speed of daily lives leaves us too often breathless and torn.

So do unexplainable tragedies.

The uniting of spirits with kindred souls

Helps rekindle basic focus on what's important.

We need others of all ages and talents for completion.

This evening's music temporarily helped

the Magnet escape torment

By allowing him to join in fellowship in true give and take.

His loneliness and hurt disappeared through the sharing.

So too did others find comfort.

We all won that night, even the dogs,

Eternal optimists,

Scrounging for scraps and fellowship they know are left for them.

Eventually, the music stopped as the Magnet's force lessened.

All the better for the experience, and

Knowing we'd find our way back,

We left.

Written about a night spent in northern Iredell County listening to Ray Cline and other wonderful musicians playing in the Douglass farmhouse sometime in the winter of 2001.

Poetry Nuzzles

Readers puzzle

While poets dazzle

Using words in nifty combos

To present us in our worldly surroundings.

Sometimes there's lots of wow and pow—

Sometimes only a dull ho hum—

Yet poetry's always a meaningful experience,

Frequently causing cranial upheaval.

Good poetry

Wanders through heads,

Dribbling tidbits of life and

Forcing sensual experiences upon us.

Laughter, tears, anger, boredom,

Witty observations, lust, tough questions,

Itchy-twitchy feelings, war, or love:

Verse explores all.

Maybe poets' ponderings

Lead us to better understandings

Of our daily meanderings.

Wow Factor

Writers come and go.

Some few leave kernels to grow

While others just disappear

With little to show.

Thoughts, not words,

Tangle, tripping most

Unable to tiptoe through the

Twisted vines cluttering a chosen way.

Crisp clarity cries in triumph

When a rare, well-written work

Escapes murky mazes of convoluted thought and

Creates a lasting wow factor.

Suddenly readers glean an image or expression

That dazzles and lasts.

It is the Holy Grail,

Too often sought and too rarely found.